S0-BRS-915

Retzel

REACHING CHILDREN

REACHING CHILDREN

By

MILDRED MORNINGSTAR

MOODY PRESS
153 Institute Place
Chicago, Ill.

Copyright, 1944, by
The Moody Bible Institute
of Chicago

Printed in the United States of America

DEDICATED

To my father, H. A. Whaley, whose interest and encouragement helped make this book a possibility.

FOREWORD

The winning of boys and girls to Jesus Christ and leading them in growth in grace is engaging the lives of Christians today as never before. It is with the view of providing practical helps for the new teacher and workable solutions to problems for the experienced one, that this book has been written.

Some of the ideas set forth are new and original, some have been used for many years by many workers, but all have borne the test of actual trial, and have been found profitable. Many of the sources of these ideas have long since been forgotten, but grateful acknowledgment is hereby given to each one. It is with the prayer that these "tips" shall prove of real value to the teachers of boys and girls that this book is set forth.

MILDRED MORNINGSTAR

CONTENTS

1

INVITING THE CHILD TO CHRIST

THE change in attitude toward the giving of the invitation to boys and girls to accept the Saviour as their own, is enough to gladden the heart of every born-again believer. Mothers, who have prayed long years over their wayward sons, and fathers, who have grieved because of transgressing daughters, might have new hope if their yesterdays could be lived today. Yesterday, the bringing of a boy or girl to a decision to accept Christ was most frequently left to the visiting evangelist, or to the pastor who conducted a special decision service for the Sunday school—the parents doing their part by seeing that their children attended the meetings. Today, it is being seen that this work of bringing children to Christ is not for the evangelist or pastor alone, but that the mother or father, the Sunday school teacher, the adult who has never before done anything for his Lord, the new convert—in fact, any believer may have a part in bringing boys and girls to an actual decision to accept Christ.

It has been found that sometimes those who have never taught children make the best soul winners of boys and girls. New joy has come to them. Older women, ready almost for a permanent appointment with the rocking chair and knitting needles have been thrilled and their lives transformed when they found

11

that the Lord Jesus had a place for them in His vine-
yard—that they could win the children in their
neighborhood to a real knowledge of Christ as
Saviour. Yes, even high school girls, glowing with
love for their new-found Saviour, have discovered an
avenue of service, a new purpose in their lives and a
radiant joy in bringing little ones to the foot of the
Cross. Just as anyone may go seek a straying lamb,
so any Christian may seek to bring a lost, little one
to the safety of Christ's fold. In fact, a whole new
ministry has opened for the average Christian—one
that brings joy and delight and thanksgiving to God
for the privilege of being used by Him.

Perhaps it might help us to better understand this
new ministry by contrasting the old and new methods
of training children in spiritual things. The old
method of approach included teaching children Bible
stories, facts about the Bible and desirable traits of
Christian conduct during the time they were young
and believing. When they became older the Sunday
school or church put on a special decision service or
evangelistic campaign in which the way of salvation
was presented, and the children asked to respond by
receiving the Lord as their personal Saviour. Thus
the child possessed much Bible knowledge, and
knowledge of what was right and wrong, before he
ever knew the gospel of the saving grace of God.
Under the old method the invitation came at the
climax of much Bible training and teaching.

The old method is still the policy in many places,
but there has been an awakening on the part of alert
Christian leaders all over the country to a new
method of bringing children to a knowledge of the
Lord.

The new method consists in presenting *first of all* the most vital of all Bible truths, the way of salvation, and giving the child an opportunity to receive the Saviour then. Subsequent lessons seek to teach him to live for the Lord Jesus, and to establish him in the knowledge of the Word. Thus the invitation is placed at the beginning instead of at the climax of a series of lessons.

Many children, who only occasionally drop into the Bible class or Sunday school may not only be evangelized, but may truly be saved if this modern plan is followed. Under the old plan they might not happen to be present on the day when the way of salvation was presented, and perhaps, therefore, left to wander years in sin before they finally heard the simple way to be freed from sin.

However, this was not the case with black-eyed eight-year-old Glen who came with his cousin, Ella, to Sunday school on Thanksgiving Sunday for the first time. The teacher breathed a quick prayer that he might see the Saviour on that one day he was visiting. She adapted the lesson, and put more emphasis on the way of salvation than she had planned, for all the other children were saved. When she gave the invitation, Glen's hand shot up without a second's hesitation. He eagerly asked Jesus into his heart. The teacher then mentioned certain spiritual blessings that became ours the moment we received Jesus as Saviour, and as one was mentioned, she asked who would like to thank Jesus for it. Glen's black eyes shone as he realized the blessings that were his in Christ, and it was his hand that was always up before the rest. He had visited one Sunday, heard, and accepted the way of salvation, and went on his way rejoicing. If the old method had been followed, Glen would have heard one of a series of lessons which lead ultimately to presenting salvation, but his one visit with the Sunday school would not have brought to him a personal knowledge of the Saviour. This method of seizing every opportunity to show children the way to be saved, and inviting them to come to the Lord, results in the salvation of many more boys and girls.

Then, too, this repetition of the way of salvation has its effect upon the regular members of the class. They become more familiar with God's way of saving folks—they are not surprised when someone responds to the giving of the invitation. In fact, they come to expect the newcomers and visitors to be saved. In the instance previously mentioned, when the invitation was given, the rest of the boys and girls listened reverently, but not one of them responded. They were saved, and they knew it. This was a procedure familiar to them. The frequency with which it occurred impressed firmly on their minds and hearts just what was necessary to believe in order to be saved, and it was manifested in their daily lives. Corinne, whose black, curly hair, deep blue eyes and fair skin would have been the answer to many a mother's prayer, was also a keen cause for thanksgiving on the part of her teacher. Each Sunday she would report about some child to whom she had talked during the week. If he said he did not believe it when she told how to be saved, she would read him her memory verses out of her small black Bible. "What shall I tell him now?" she would ask earnestly, and the sincerity of this eight-year-old soul winner was another sign that God approved of the emphasis laid on the gospel and the invitation.

After all, the things we hear most frequently are the ones that we never forget, for they have become a very part of us. If someone asked you the chief products or industries of Bolivia, or some other far-away country you once studied in school, you might not be able to remember. But if the same person asked you, "What is five times six?" you would give the answer without hesitation. Why the difference? The ones who planned the school curriculum knew that the latter fact was something you would need to know throughout life; therefore it was taught with such emphasis, and with so much repetition that you could not forget it. And is not the gospel of just as much importance as the multiplication table? If we believe it, it will be a help to us all through life, and in the end carry us safely into a blissful eternity. Oh, let us as teachers, as Christian parents and friends of little children see that this vital truth is made so important and so impressive to the little ones that they shall never, never forget it.

Another advantage of presenting the gospel with the invitation each time, is that absentees will not miss the opportunity to be saved as they otherwise might. One of the writer's keenest disappointments came when following the old method in teaching a primary group in Daily Vacation Bible School. It was my first experience with children of this age, and I prayed earnestly that I might lead them to Christ. The last Friday's lesson was on the crucifixion; therefore I planned on that day to give them the way of salvation, and to have a decision service in our class. Ordinarily there were nine or ten children present out of an enrolment of twelve. The last day finally came. I had prayed that there would be a good attendance, but the Lord had something He wanted to teach me. The night before, there was a regular downpour, and the rural roads were deep in mud. Lack of suitable clothing kept many of the children away, and it was with a sinking heart that I saw only six in my class that morning. True, all six responded when we read from God's Word how to be saved, and they all sweetly asked to be saved when we had a time of prayer. The other six who were absent were just as willing as those who were present. They passed out of my class where they had been for two weeks, knowing a few Bible stories, a few memory verses, but ignorant as to the most vital fact of all. They did not know how to be saved. What a tragedy! I never saw those children again. I do not yet know whether or not they are saved, but I do know that I learned a lesson that I shall never forget. Since then I have taught many classes in Daily Vacation Bible Schools. But now I seek to win as many as possible on the first day, others on the second and third days, and to concentrate the remainder of the time on the newcomers and visitors. It is very rare that any regular attendants slip through without coming to a definite decision for Christ. At least not one can say, "You never told me how to be saved."

There is another danger that may be avoided by giving the gospel and the invitation frequently. It lessens the likelihood of many children growing up in the Sunday school and church, and yet not being regenerated. The average man or woman outside the church looks upon the regular attendants as Christians. Of course, we know that this does not necessarily follow. True regeneration is a matter of the heart, and not of outward observances. Nevertheless, these unsaved regular attendants whose lives have never known the transforming power of the Lord become a stumbling block to their friends and neighbors. Their attitude is, "Why should I become a Christian, or why should I go to church—I'm better than he is." And the worst of it is, that this is very often true.

A missionary from Africa once told me that this very thing had caused one of their greatest problems. Many children were brought up in the missionary schools which had been established to aid in the education of the country, but never received Christ as their Saviour. The other natives looked upon them as Christians, but when these educated, unsaved natives went back to their villages, it was often to cheat, and to take advantage of the others. You can easily see the problem this would create for the missionaries. This missionary admitted that their emphasis had been on education rather than on evangelism. Of course, it is not our responsibility to force others to accept Christ, but it is our duty to see that each child has the message presented to him in a way that he understands, and that he is given an opportunity to receive Christ. The great advantage of following this course with children is that a great percentage of them will be touched with the message, and will be eager to accept the Lord.

Thus, we have seen that following the new method will bring more children to the Lord, including visitors and absentees, will build up and establish the regular members of the class, and will to a large degree prevent the children from growing up to be a stumbling block to those outside the church.

THE CHILD'S WILLINGNESS

Long ago the Saviour said, "Go out into the highways and hedges, and compel them to come in" (Luke 14:23). Did He mean that by the time they were grown there were so many outside interests in the lives of these people that they were no longer desirous of coming to Him, and that strong measures had to be used if they should come to Him at all? But what did He say of the children? "Let the little children come to me; . . . do not hinder them" (Luke 18:16, Weymouth translation). It was almost as if He had said, "Cease being a hindrance to the children—get out of the way—and they will come to me. They are different from the hardened adults."

If Jesus Christ, God's Son, called the children, who are we to say that they should not be given the invitation to salvation? The Son still desires their fellowship. Of the Father He said, "It is not the will of your Father which is in heaven, that one of these little ones should perish" (Matt. 18:14).

Workers who follow the plan suggested—that of giving the gospel to the children first, and then following it with an invitation to accept Christ—are amazed by the eagerness with which the children listen and respond to the gospel. A young married woman taught her first child evangelism class and reported to the teacher of the training class. "Yes, we had twelve dear little children. I had no helper but really we got along fine. I'm not quite sure I did everything right," she added questioningly.

"Did you follow the general plan of the hour? Fifteen minutes for singing, fifteen minutes for memory work, with twenty minutes for the story and the balance of the time for the invitation and closing prayer?" asked the teacher.

"Oh, yes, I did. But when I gave the invitation, all twelve children wanted to be saved! That is what made me wonder if I had done it right."

"If the children wanted to be saved, you must have conducted the hour correctly. For that is the purpose of the class. Many of these children have never heard the gospel before they come to the class. Their consciences are tender; they realize their sinfulness, and desire to be saved when they hear the way."

But we doubting adults say, "They are so small. Can they really understand?"

Who, may I ask, completely understands God's plan of salvation? Surely it is founded on love, and Paul, one of the most learned men of all time, calls it "the love of Christ which passeth knowledge." The mind of the greatest philosopher of all ages cannot fully comprehend what God does when He saves a soul, or to what depths Christ had to go in order to purchase our redemption. It is beyond human comprehension. No, the little child cannot understand these mysteries. What, then, is necessary? Only to believe, in the full sense of the word.

John 3:16: "For God so loved the world, that he gave his only begotten Son, that whosoever *believeth in him* . . . " He does not say, "Whosoever understandeth," or "whosoever is able to explain it," but "whosoever believeth." Who is more believing than a little child? Let us give them the gospel while they are young and believing.

GIVING THE CHILD THE GOSPEL

Just what is the gospel? It is the good news "that Christ died for our sins according to the scriptures; and that he was buried, and that he rose again the third day according to the scriptures" (I Cor. 15: 3, 4). This good news of the way of salvation divides itself into three parts:

1. Man's need—he is lost.
2. God's provision—He sent His Son, Jesus, to die for lost mankind.
3. Acceptance by faith for salvation—man must receive Christ's work by faith in order to be saved.

In other words, to be saved I must:

1. Believe that I am a sinner.
2. Believe that Christ died for my sins.
3. Believe that when I ask Him, He comes into my heart.

Or, to state it another way, I must:

1. Recognize the fact of my personal sin.
2. Realize in my heart that Jesus died for that sin.
3. Receive Him as my personal Saviour.

The Bible abounds in passages proving this and explaining it.

MEMORY WORK

1. Sin—Rom. 3:10; 3:23; Isa. 53:6; 64:6; Jer. 17:9.
2. Christ's death for sin—I Cor. 15:3, 4; I Pet. 2:24; Isa. 53:6; Rom. 5:6, 8.
3. He must be personally received—Rev. 3:20; John 1:12; 3:16; 3:18; 3:36; I John 5:12.

We ourselves need to have a clear conception of the gospel in order to present it to the children. Let the teacher study the foregoing outlines on the way of salvation, until they become a very part of her. How many Scripture passages can you find on each one of them? Do you notice how man's work is omitted? Our works are not acceptable in God's sight for salvation.

Ephesians 2:8, 9: "For by grace are ye saved through faith; and that not of yourselves: it is the gift of God: Not of works, lest any man should boast." Titus 3:5: "Not by works of righteousness which we have done, but according to his mercy he saved us, by the washing of regeneration, and renewing of the Holy Ghost."

All the plans of salvation propagated by all the religions in the world can be reduced to just two:

1. Salvation is by grace, the free gift of God, or
2. Salvation is by works which are acceptable to God.

The Lord, knowing how universal the plan of salvation by works would become, put in His Word, in the opening chapters of Genesis, an object lesson to show us which plan was acceptable to Him.

There were two boys. Each brought an offering to God, which tells us that God must have made known His will regarding offerings. Cain brought an offering of his good works—part of his crop. But Abel brought of the firstlings of his flock. He brought a life, and the blood was shed—the blood of another. "And the Lord had respect unto Abel and his offering: But unto Cain and to his offering he had not respect" (Gen. 4:4, 5). Abel was received, because his bringing a lamb showed that his faith was placed in the offering of another for his sin. "By faith Abel offered unto God a more excellent sacrifice than Cain, by which he obtained witness that he was righteous" (Heb. 11:4). Abel illustrates the group of those who rely for salvation on the death of another, while Cain stands for the class which presents good works to God for salvation.

Boys and girls, however, are taught from their earliest days that they should be good—which is right and proper. They are taught that God does not love bad boys, and that if they are not good they will not go to heaven. Thus early in life children have the idea of salvation by works. All of which makes a very good club to hold over the child's head, but which happens not to be true. God *does* love bad boys. If He didn't He would have no one to love, for we are all bad. Romans 3:23: "For all have sinned, and come short of the glory of God." Romans 5:8: "But God commendeth his love toward us, in that, while we were yet sinners, Christ died for us." John 3:16: "For God so loved the *world* (including bad boys and girls), that he gave his only begotten Son . . ."

Notice that it is a matter of believing—not of imploring God to save us. We do not have to make God willing to save us from sin. He is willing already. So willing that He sent His Son "to seek and to save that which was lost." The moment we turn to Him we are found. Salvation does not need to be an agonizing experience. Like the prodigal's father, God is so willing that He has already come out to meet us. Our part is to come to Him. When this is explained to little children, they are eager to accept the Lord as their own Saviour. We must be careful, however, to see that each part of the gospel is made plain, so that our work will not be superficial. If the following plan is followed, the chances for having decisions without real heart experiences will be greatly minimized.

The Gospel in the Story

As you tell the story to the boys and girls see that it contains the three points of the way of salvation. Ask yourself these questions. Where can I best bring out the matter of sin, that the boys and girls listening might know that they are sinners? Many classes begin with the wordless book. The matter of sin is easily introduced in this lesson. As soon as the black page is mentioned, we have the problem of sin. And so it should be in every story. Sin should be shown as that which separates us from God (Isa. 59:2). If it is not mentioned in the story, use an illustration, perhaps from your own childhood, which fits in and shows the fact of sin. Get the children *lost* before you try to get them saved.

A great deal depends upon the teacher's attitude as to whether or not boys and girls will be willing to admit their lost condition. If she points her finger at them and says severely, "You children have sinned. You know you have. You have all done wrong. You need to be saved, or you will never go to heaven. Now, haven't you sinned?" Little heads will vigor-ously shake in the negative. But if the teacher is will-ing to admit herself a sinner and take a sympathetic attitude toward the children, it becomes easier for them to admit their own guilt. The story of some sin committed in the teacher's own childhood, with the spiritual application drawn from it will do much to show the children that their teacher is human. Many children have the idea that I had when a child— that children are sinners, but adults are perfect. Therefore, they try to keep their guilt hid from the adult. The teacher might say, "Yes, boys and girls, just this one sin would have been enough to keep me out of heaven. But Jesus loved me just as He loves all those who have done wrong, and He died for my sin so that I might be saved. If Jesus had not died I never could have gone to heaven."

It also helps to tell the children that all have sinned, all have done wrong. All the Sunday school teachers, the ministers, the mothers, the fathers, the big boys and girls, and little ones, too. This will come as a shock to some children. It helps them realize that others are in the same predicament as they.

In telling a Bible story which speaks of some character's sin, the teacher might insert this application with the story:

"Boys and girls, we all get dirty. There is not a person living who does not get dirty, and does not need a bath. It is not a shame to get dirty, but it would be a shame to stay dirty, to never wash or take a bath. That would be a disgrace. Just the same way, it is not a disgrace to be a sinner, for we all have sinned. But it is a disgrace to stay that way, and never let Jesus wash our sins away in His precious blood."

The above suggestions are given to be used during the story to make clear the first point.

What is the next point of the way of salvation? "That Christ died for our sins according to the scriptures." In telling the story of the wordless book, this comes under the red page. But in telling other Bible stories, you may not so clearly see the connection to the Cross. Look for it closely for it will surely be there. Calvary is the theme of the Bible; in every book it is either declared, or hidden in type. Claim the promise in John 16:14 spoken of the Holy Spirit: "He shall glorify me: for he shall receive of mine, and shall shew it unto you." Part of the office work of the Holy Spirit is to reveal Christ unto us. As we come with open hearts unto the Word of God we will see Christ anew in His sacrificial work upon the Cross of Calvary, even in passages we did not dream contained this message. It will then be our privilege to seek to make real to the children Christ's death for sin. Let us always be sure that our story contains somewhere the truth of Jesus dying on the cross, for there is no salvation without His cross-work.

Illustrations are the windows of the message— they let in the light. A house is not all windows, and yet it would not be complete without a few. Just so with the Bible story for children. An apt illustration helps to emphasize the point, and to make it clear to the listener. Of course, the "point" in this case is the gospel.

The stories which follow have been very effective in making clear the substitutionary work of Christ. They are not given to be used by themselves—boys and girls need *Bible* stories—but they are to be incorporated into the story at the place where the teacher brings out the second point of the gospel, "Christ died for our sins," to show the boys and girls that He gave Himself to save us.

The Hen and Her Chickens *good*

Once upon a time there were twelve tiny, yellow balls of fluff. "Peep, peep, peep." They went in and out of their mother's legs, under her wings, up on top of her back, two or three feet away, and then back again. Guess what they were? That's right, they were little baby chicks. Their mother, Biddy, clucked to them. She would hold little pieces of food in her beak, and try to feed them. If Billy would come near the barn where they lived, she would ruffle up her feathers, and if he would pick up one of her babies, she would cluck ferociously. Biddy didn't want any-thing to happen to them, for she loved them.

But one day when Billy and his father and mother were gone, something terrible happened. The barn caught on fire, and when they came home, it was smoking, and all black. One side had fallen in. Billy and his father went into the barn. The door was all black, and it made Billy's hands black when he touched it. There was the place where the straw had been; it was just a little pile of ashes now. Over in the corner they saw a little, dark shape.

"Why, that looks just like a hen," said Billy.

"Listen," said Daddy. "I hear something."

"Peep, peep, peep."

Billy ran over to the dark shape. He touched it with his foot. It fell over. But out came some little chickens climbing all over each other.

"Why, that was a hen," said Billy. "That was Biddy. But she is all burned. She is dead."

"Yes," said Daddy.

"But when the fire came, why didn't she fly out the window there? Even if the door was shut, she could have gone out the window."

"Yes, but her baby chicks couldn't fly. They would all have been burned to death. I'm sure Biddy knew that, and clucked to her babies when the fire came so that each one got underneath her wings. She loved them more than she loved herself. She wanted to save them. So the fire burned her, but the chicks were saved. That reminds me of what Jesus did," said Daddy.

"How is that?" and Billy looked puzzled.

"Jesus knew we could not save ourselves. We have all sinned, and so He said to God, 'I will be punished for their sins.' He did not need to die on the cross. He could have come down, but He wanted to save us. He had to die to do it, just like Biddy had to die to save her chicks."

"I guess I'm just like one of these baby chicks. Jesus knew I would have to die, so He died for me. Is that right?"

"Yes, it is. He loved you so much He died for you."

"Oh, I'm glad He did that. I know I have done wrong, and I do want to be saved."

"Let's tell Jesus right now," said Daddy.

Billy knelt down right on the black floor. "Oh, Jesus, I didn't know you died for me. I'm so glad you loved me that much. Please save me right now."

After that, every time Billy saw a hen he remembered Biddy, and thanked Jesus again because He had given His life to save him.

Bobby and the Ruler *good*

One story that never fails to interest and impress children has as its setting one familiar to all children —the schoolroom.

It was two o'clock in the afternoon, and all the boys and girls in the room had just finished their reading lesson. Miss Johnson stood up in front of them and said severely, "I want every boy and girl to sit up very straight. Get your reading books, and read tomorrow's lesson. I am going out of the room, and

I do not want anyone to whisper while I am gone."
She shook her finger as she looked straight at the
children.

Bobby sat in a front seat. He could hear the clock
go "Tick, tock, tick, tock," the room was so quiet.
He wondered how long Miss Johnson would be gone.
He started to read the lesson, but pretty soon he
thought about what he was going to do after school,
and he leaned across the aisle, and whispered to his
pal, Jimmy. Jimmy listened to what he had to say,
but did not say anything back. Just then Miss Johnson came back into the room. "Did anyone whisper
while I was gone?" and she looked over the whole
room.

"Oh, dear," thought Bobby, "why did I whisper?"
His heart sank clear down into his shoes. But he
wasn't a coward. Up went little Bobby's hand.

"Did you whisper while I was gone?"

"Yes, ma'am," said Bobby, swallowing hard.

"Then come with me to the principal's office, and
get your punishment."

Just then a hand waved in the back of the room.

"Yes, Tom, what is it?"

"Please, Miss Johnson," and big, twelve-year-old
Tom stood up. "Bobby is such a little boy, and he
doesn't feel very good. I know, because I live next
door to him. Please, Miss Johnson, couldn't I take his
punishment for him?"

"Did you whisper, Tom?"

"No ma'am, I didn't."

"And you want the principal to punish you instead of Bobby?"

"Yes ma'am."

"Then both of you come with me to the principal's office."

Little seven-year-old Bobby, and big Tom walked down the empty hall around the corner to the school office.

Mr. Turner looked up when they came in.

"Mr. Turner," said Miss Johnson, "I am sorry, but it is necessary to have you punish Tom."

"Why, Tom, you surprise me, you have such a good record. I have never had to punish you before."

He opened his desk drawer, took out a long ruler, and walked toward Tom. Bobby sat down on a chair and watched.

"Hold out your hand."

Tom stretched out his hand, the principal raised the ruler. He brought it down hard on the palm of Tom's hand. One stroke. Tom winced. The principal raised the ruler again. Down it came—two strokes! Three! Four! Five!

By this time there were tears in Tom's eyes. Bobby saw them, and he blinked too. But the principal kept right on. Six! Seven! Eight! Nine! Ten! Bobby could stand it no longer. He grabbed Tom around the neck, and burst out crying.

"Oh, Tom, thank you, thank you! You weren't bad. I was the one. Thank you! 'N' you can have my roller skates, 'n' you can have my bicycle, 'n' my football, 'n' anything I have. 'N' we'll be pals forever 'n' ever!"

Tom being punished for Bobby was just like Jesus dying on the cross for us, boys and girls. We were the ones who were bad, but He loved us, and let God punish Him for our sins. Won't you believe that He loved you that much, and won't you receive

Him as your own personal Saviour? Won't you tell Him that you are glad that He died for you? Won't you be friends with Him forever and ever?

The story of the hen and chicks, and of Bobby and the ruler give very apt illustrations of Christ's substitutionary death on the cross. A little tract called "The Colonel's Word Will Stand" contains another good story for making plain this important point. Watch for tracts containing stories which can be used to illustrate spiritual truths, and you can make your stories more interesting, as well as more effective. However, never use an illustration, no matter how good it is, unless it lets in the light on the point you want emphasized. To do so is to digress, to weaken your story, and to make the application less powerful.

The simple telling of the story of the crucifixion cannot be surpassed in making clear the gospel, but the foregoing illustrations may be used when most of the class is familiar with the gospel, with a few newcomers who need to have the truth presented to them.

In the same way, the third point of the way of salvation (that we must receive Christ to be saved) should be incorporated into the story, either growing out of the Bible text or introduced as an illustration. Thus we are sure that the whole gospel has been presented during the actual telling of the story.

The Gospel in the Invitation

Then, at the climax of the story, without pause or evidence that there is a change, proceed right into the invitation. Do not stop to sing a song; this confuses little children, but put the proposition to them fairly and squarely. Do not coax or plead with them, but give them a fair opportunity. If the group is a new group which has never heard the gospel before, it is less distracting not to have them bow their heads, but to deal with them in a straightforward manner. They are not familiar with Christian behaviour, and until they have been taught about prayer, it is shrouded in mystery to them. While their heads are bowed they are tempted to peek, merely wondering what is to happen next, all of which tends to distract them from the invitation. In other words, treat the invitation as a part of the story, in fact as the very climax of it.

The gospel may be summarized in the invitation. In doing this, the invitation becomes inseparably linked with the story. Summarize the way of salvation as you give it, repeating each point briefly. Can you recognize all three points?

The following are given as samples of the close of the story:

1. *After almost any story*

"Perhaps some of you boys and girls know that you have done wrong, but you are so glad to learn that Jesus died for every one of your sins, and that now He is knocking at the door of your heart, waiting for you to receive Him. If you really and truly want to let Him in, raise your hand, and I will help you to ask Him into your heart." It is easier for children to understand if you correlate the invitation with the story, using similar terminology.

2. *After the story of the three crosses*

"Boys and girls, God's Word says that we are all like these two thieves—we all have sinned. You know

that you have sinned, but you don't want to keep
your sinful heart. You want to be like the thief that
believed on Jesus and had his sins washed away. You
believe that Jesus died for your sins, and right now
you want to ask Him to save you. If you do, you may
raise your hand, and I will help you to ask Him to
save you."

3. *After the story of the wordless book*

"How many of you realize that your heart is in
darkness (turn to black page) because you have done
wrong, but you believe that Jesus shed His blood on
the cross for you (turn to red page), and you want
Him to come into your heart to make it as white as
snow (turn to white page). If you really mean it, you
may raise your hand, and I will help you to ask
Him to come in."

4. *After story of Abraham and Isaac (Genesis 22):*

"Abraham offered up his only son, Isaac. Another
Father, God, offered up His only Son, Jesus, to pay
for our sins. As Isaac carried the wood upon which
he was to be sacrificed, so Jesus carried the wooden
cross. Isaac was being obedient to his father. Jesus
was being obedient to His Father, but more than
that, He loved us and wanted to die for our sins.
Abraham tied Isaac to the altar, but there were nails
put in Jesus' hands. It was not the nails, but His love
for us that held Him to the cross. Do you believe
that Jesus died for your sins, and will you accept this
wonderful love, by taking Jesus as your own personal Saviour?"

5. *After story of the leper (Matthew 8:1-4):*

"This leper was covered with sores, and no matter
what medicine he used they would not get well. Did

you know that our hearts were sick too? We have all done wrong things, which makes our hearts so sick that nothing we can do will make them well. We might cover them up with bandages of lies, so that others might not know, but down underneath, the naughtiness is still there. No one could do anything for the leper but Jesus. No one can do anything for our sick hearts but Jesus. He just had to speak, and the sick man was made well, but He had to die on the cross in order to make our sick hearts well. Will you bring your sick heart to Jesus, tell Him that you believe He died for you, and ask Him to cleanse you from sin?"

6. *After the story of creation (Genesis 1):* ✓

"On the fourth day the Lord made the great light-holder which we call the sun. He gave it to us for a picture of His Son, Jesus, who is the Light of the world. If we had a house and had all the shades pulled, and all the doors closed so that the sunlight could not get in, it would be very dark and dreary. Our hearts are dark and dreary without Jesus, the Light of the world. But He died on the cross to take away our darkness. Now He stands outside the door of our heart, knocking. He wants to come in and make it light and cheerful. He is knocking at your door. Will you say, 'Yes, Jesus, I know my heart is dark with sin. I believe you died for me, and I now open the door to let you come in and make my heart light'?"

Do you see how the invitation may really be a part of the story? After you have tried for several times to fit the invitation to the story it will almost become second nature to you. But don't think that you are different from anyone else if you have shaking knees as you think about giving the invitation for the first time. This was the hard part for me in teaching my first class. I did not know what to say, or what to do if anyone should be saved, but I studied hard and prayed harder. The Lord brought me through and gave me the soul of each little child who was present. How I praise Him for it. And He is still the same Lord.

The Gospel in the After-Meeting

Up to this time the three points of the way of salvation have been presented in the story, and summarized in the invitation, but now they should be applied individually in the after-meeting. Now the after-meeting need not be that at all. But for want of a better name we label thus the period when the children are dealt with as to receiving the Lord. At this time each part of the way of salvation is reviewed.

Perhaps you have a new class. You give the invitation, and seven out of the nine children present raise their hands indicating that they desire to be saved. To have the children go into another room would be folly—practically the whole group would follow you there. The thing to do is to deal with them as they are. The three points must be again presented to them, to see that each one individually believes each one. What are they? First, I believe I am a sinner. Second, I believe that Christ died for my sins. Third, by faith I invite Him into my heart to be my Saviour.

In this little group speak confidentially to them, as one individual to another. "You boys and girls

have said that you want to be saved. There is just
one way to be saved. First of all, we must know that
we have done wrong. Then we must believe that
Jesus Christ, God's Son, died for our sins, and last
of all we must invite Him into our hearts. It says in
the Bible, right here, 'all have sinned.' " If some of
the children are old enough, have one of them read
the first four words of Romans 3:23 from your Bible
which you hand to him, with the four words under-
lined.

"Now, God says that all have sinned, and He
knows because He can see right down into our hearts.
Do you boys and girls believe that you have sinned?"
If the group is small, ask each one individually, but
if there are twenty-five or more, have them raise their
hands. If one of the children does not admit his guilt
do not deal with him then, but tell him you will talk
with him afterwards, and proceed to deal with the
willing ones.

After each willing one has admitted that he is a
sinner, turn in your Bible to I Corinthians 15:3.

"Now, children, God sent Jesus to die for our
sins. It says so in His Word. I will read it to you.
'Christ died for our sins.' That means that because
I was bad Christ died for my sins. That means that
because you were bad Christ died for your sins. He
let them put the nails into His hands because He
wanted to pay for your sins. God punished Him for
each sin I have committed, and for each one I ever
will commit. Jesus paid for them all because He loved
us so. Do you boys and girls believe that? Jane, do
you believe that Jesus died for all your sins? Henry,
do you?" Get each child to tell you that he believes
that Jesus died for him, either by raising his hand in

the case of a very large group, or by continuing to ask each one individually.

"Now, boys and girls, after Jesus died God raised Him up, and now He lives in heaven, but He wants a home down here on earth in our hearts. Do you know what He is doing now? He is knocking at the door of our hearts, pleading with us to let Him come in so that He can take away our sins. He says in His Word, 'Behold I stand at the door and knock.' " Knock on a chair or nearby wall. "He is knocking because He wants to come in, but the only way He will come in is for us to ask Him. Some people say, 'No, Jesus, I don't want you in my heart,' but others say, 'Oh, Jesus, I'm so glad you loved me enough to die on the cross for my sins. I'll open the door right now, and you may come into my heart.' Do you boys and girls want to receive Him into your heart? You do? All right, we will ask Him right now. If I were at the door of your house knocking because I wanted to come in, would it be very *hard* for you to ask me to come in? Why, no. It wouldn't be hard at all, would it? Jesus is even more real than I am. He is knocking, and He wants you to let Him come in, so each one of us will ask Him. When we talk to Jesus, we bow our heads and shut our eyes. We will start with Katherine (one of the more attentive, less timid children). While we all have our heads bowed Katherine will ask Jesus to come into her heart, right out loud." Even if her prayer isn't eloquent, if it is sincere it is sufficient for salvation. Proceed around the circle, having each one pray in his own words. This has been used in a group when as many as thirty children desired to receive Christ and it is possible to have each one pray individually. Instead of calling on them or going in an orderly way around the group, you may ask who wants to ask Jesus next; thus you deal with the most willing ones first. However, this may be determined at the time you are dealing with the group. Use whichever method seems to be more suitable.

This may be more work and take extra time, but the children thus dealt with will be clear on each point of the way of salvation, and it will amaze you to watch their growth in grace. If this seems entirely too difficult for you, you may have the children in a group repeat after you a simple prayer with the instructions to do so only if they are in earnest. Repeat the prayer first so they will understand and then have them say it phrase by phrase. A prayer such as the following could be used: "Dear Jesus, I believe that I have sinned. Thank you for dying for my sins. Come into my heart right now and save me. Amen."

Remember, if an unusually large number of children desire to be saved at one meeting, you can call at any time on the Lord for special wisdom, and He will give it. "If any of you lack wisdom, let him ask of God, that giveth to all men liberally, and upbraideth not" (James 1:5).

If it is possible to take more time, the suggestions that follow will bring immeasurable help to the child and will do a great deal to insure his having a healthy Christian life. If it is not possible, do not be discouraged. Remember that now the child is saved he is in God's family, and that God is able to care for His own children.

Immediately after the child has prayed, ask him, "Who is in your heart now?" "Who paid for your sins?" "Do you have to pay for them?" "What does

this verse say you are?" Read Acts 16:31. "Whose
child are you now?" (John 1:12). Try to correlate
these questions with the line of approach used in
the invitation. For instance, in presenting Jesus as
the light, ask, "Are you in darkness anymore?"
"Why not?" "What is Jesus?" (The Light of the
world.) "Where is He?" (In my heart.)

After the children have asked God to save them,
seek to awaken in them a spirit of thankfulness.
When you see by their faces that they do appreciate
what Jesus has done for them, ask, "Who would like
to thank Jesus because He died on the cross and
saved you?" What joy it will give you as one by one
they eagerly give thanks to their new-found Saviour.
Let the words be their own even if they are ever so
simple. One little boy just bowed his head and said
softly, "Thank you, Jesus." I am sure that was
sweeter music in the ears of our Lord than many a
more eloquent prayer. The prayer of praise does a
great deal in giving the child the assurance that is so
vital for Christian growth.

Tell the child also that Jesus has saved him from
sin, and that He will keep him from sinning if he
asks Him. If, however, he should forget and do something wrong, he should tell Jesus about it at once,
saying that he is sorry, and that he would trust Jesus
to help him not to do it the next time. "If we confess
our sins, he is faithful and just to forgive us our sins,
and to cleanse us from all unrighteousness" (I John
1:9).

If given to the child when he is first saved, these
three things that Jesus wants us to do will greatly

aid him in his Christian life. If there is time in the after-meeting the teacher might say:

"We have found out today how much Jesus has done for us. Did you know that there were three things that He wants us to do for Him? The first one is to read His Word. (Hold up your Bible.) This is His letter to us. When we read it, it is like Jesus talking right to us. If we want to know what He wants us to do, we can find out in the Bible. He wants us to read it every day. If it is hard for you to read, ask your mother or your big brother or sister to help you, but remember not to go to bed at night until you have heard what Jesus has to say."

If they do not have a Bible, give them penny portions of Psalms or one of the Gospels from the American Bible Society. This might be supplemented later on with a ten cent booklet, "Daily Bread," by J. Irvin Overholtzer. Allow the child to earn this booklet as it is a bad policy to give out too much material. "The Children's Guide Book" contains no marks which would designate it as belonging to any one church. It is good to give to children who have only heard the gospel once or twice, because it reviews it in simple language and gives instructions for the Christian life. "Six Wonderful Things" tells of six things that happen the moment a child accepts Christ. It is effective where children have been under the sound of the gospel for some time before accepting Christ.

"The next thing He wants us to do is to talk to Him. What would you think if I asked you to come into my house and never said a word to you? Would you think I loved you very much? Now, Jesus lives in you, and He wants you to talk to Him, and tell

Him all your troubles, for He will help you. If you have a hard lesson at school ask Jesus to help you and He will, every time. Then tell Him about the good times you have too, and talk to Him just because you love Him. 'If ye shall ask anything in my name, I will do it' (John 14:14).

"The last thing is the hardest of all, but Jesus will help us do it. That is to tell someone else that we believe in Jesus.

"Today we have read the Bible, we have prayed, or talked to Jesus, but we haven't told anyone that we believe in Jesus. I wonder who will be brave enough to stand up and tell us that you believe in Jesus? Reading the Bible is like eating, it helps us to grow bigger, and praying is like breathing, and telling someone else about Jesus is like taking exercise, it gives us good muscles."

Some of the most glorious moments of my life have been those spent in listening to little boys and girls speak out their faith in Christ immediately after they accepted Him. How their faces light up with the joy of heaven.

Great care must be exercised in certain strict Jewish or Catholic communities in the giving out of gospel literature. To give earmarked literature to the child may mean he will never return because of his parents. Big classes have dwindled to nothing overnight because young leaders unwisely gave tracts to the children. In such cases it is perhaps better to establish the child in the class, and to call on the home before giving out literature. Let the Holy Spirit be your guide in these antagonistic communities. If at all possible, the child should have a portion of God's Word.

Some have objected to telling the child that it is hard to tell others of Jesus. But it is hard! Should we shield them from the truth? If you have ninety to ninety-five percent new converts stand up immediately and testify, then don't tell them it is hard. But if you don't have that large a percentage, tell them it is hard. Ask them to trust in Christ for strength, and see what the results are. Try both ways, and do what is best for you.

If the child follows these instructions: reading the Bible, praying and testifying, he will grow in grace rapidly, even if it should happen that you never see him again. It will never be so easy for the child to testify as when he is first saved. Testimony is like letter writing—the longer we put it off the harder it becomes. If the child gives his testimony in the meeting it will not be met with a dash of cold water as it otherwise might be. If there is just one child who accepts Christ, ask him to tell some Christian who is nearby. Proceed with him to the individual and say, "Johnny has something he wants to tell you." That way the first step of testimony is taken in favorable circumstances.

Perhaps it will be impossible to conduct as lengthy an after-meeting as this would involve. Do the best you can with the help of the Lord in the time you have, and at later meetings try to give the rest of the instructions. Let us re-state the order of procedure to be followed when a child has indicated his desire to be saved.

1. Teacher reviews three points of the way of salvation, making sure each child believes each one.
2. Child prays asking the Lord to come in to save him.
3. Teacher questions child to give assurance.

4. Child thanks the Lord.
5. Teacher instructs on confession of sin.
6. Teacher instructs on "Three Things Jesus Wants You to Do."
    a. Read Bible
    b. Pray
    c. Testify
7. Child gives testimony.
8. Teacher gives child Scripture portion.

In many meetings for children the workers have been distressed because some children come forward again and again. In most cases if the preceding instructions have been heeded this will not occur, as the reasons for this have been dealt with before they arise.

Why does a child do this?

He may desire to repeat a pleasant experience. Little Patty is an example. On the first Friday meeting she had eagerly accepted the Lord as her Saviour, and when she came back the next week, she said to the teacher, "Do you remember what we did last week?" Her eyes lit up and her face beamed as she thought of it. "Let's do it all over again." The experience had been such a joyous one, she desired to repeat it. A few words of explanation from the teacher showed her that when we are saved we have happy times by talking with the Lord Jesus, instead of asking Him into our hearts again. This can be effectively illustrated by making the following supposition.

"Patty, suppose that one day I should go to see you. I knock on the front door. You look out the window and see who it is. Then you open the door and say, 'Come in, Mrs. Morningstar, I'm so glad to see you.' I sit down expecting to have a nice visit with you, but instead of that, I see you going to the door again. You open the door, and call, 'Come in, Mrs. Morningstar, come in!' What would I think?" Generally, the children laugh, see the point, and never again respond to the invitation. They see that it is a matter now of fellowshipping with the Lord Jesus, rather than of inviting Him in over and over again.

He may not be saved. He may respond to the invitation the second time because he was not really saved the first time. This does occur frequently when no after-meeting is held. The child perhaps was willing the first time. The message may not have been quite clear to him. Talk to him sympathetically and if you find this is the case, follow the steps given for dealing with an unsaved child.

He may not have the assurance of his salvation. This child should not be overlooked or dismissed because he has responded to the invitation before; he should be helped. You might proceed to help him in the following manner.

"Jack, did you ever ask Jesus to come into your heart? Is Jesus really in your heart?" He probably will say he doesn't know. "Sonny, did you really mean it when you asked Him to come in?"

"Yes, I did, but I don't know if He really came or not."

"Well, let's see what He said. The reason we know He wants to come in is because He tells us so when He knocks at our door." Turn in your Bible to Revelation 3:20. Sit beside the child so that he may see also. "Now this is what Jesus said. It was so important that He put it right in the Bible. 'If any man hear my voice, and open the door' . . . Now you knew that Jesus wanted to come in, didn't you? And when you asked Him to come in that was just the same as opening the door. So did you do what Jesus says here? Yes, you did; didn't you? All right, now we'll read what Jesus said He would do if you opened the door."

"I will come in." Let the child read it for himself. "This is actually what Jesus Christ said. Do you suppose that He would tell you a lie? I should say not! He is God; He cannot lie. So if He said that He would come in if you opened the door, and you opened the door, what did He do?" Get the child to say, "He came in."

"That is right, now where is He?"

"He's in my heart."

"Yes, aren't you glad? Jesus is perfect, and yet He will come and live in our hearts. Now, we want to find out how long He is going to stay. He tells us right in the Bible. Here it is. Hebrews 13:5: 'I will never leave you.' There is one word for each finger. Now, when will Jesus leave you?" Let him read the verse, and find it for himself.

"Never."

"Isn't that wonderful? Now, when our mother or our father does something nice for us, we thank them. Wouldn't you like to thank Jesus because He has come to live in your heart?" Have the child bow his head and in his own words thank the Son of God for taking up His abode with him.

In this way the child is dealt with on the basis of God's Word. He is basing his salvation on something that will not pass away. Too often someone is inclined to believe he is saved because he "feels good." Feelings are not permanent. The only time in the Bible a decision was based on feelings was the time

Isaac felt Jacob to determine whether or not he was Esau. His conclusion was wrong. Let us get the children to see that they are saved because God has said so in His Word. "Thy word, O Lord, is settled in heaven."

He may be out of fellowship because of sin. The child sensing that something is wrong because he has sinned may respond to the invitation thinking he needs to be saved over again. The teacher should first of all make sure that he is saved and has the assurance. She may then turn to I John 1:9: "If we confess our sins, he is faithful and just to forgive us our sins, and to cleanse us from all unrighteousness." She should explain this simply, perhaps using also Isaiah 59:2: "But your iniquities have separated between you and your God, and your sins have hid his face from you."

"When we accept Jesus as our Saviour, God becomes our Father. Just as we are happy with our father when we do what he tells us, so we are happy with God when we obey Him. But when we sin it is like disobeying our father. We do not want him to come home, and when we do see him, we are unhappy and do not want to talk with him. Our sin has spoiled everything. What should we do? We should go to our daddy, tell him what we did, and ask him to forgive us. Then we will be happy again. That is exactly what we should do when we sin. We should go to our Heavenly Father, tell Him exactly what we have done, and ask Him to forgive us. He promised in this verse He would forgive us." Have the child read the verse. Ask him then, if he is a small child (nine or under), what he has done. Ask him to tell God about it. Let him pray aloud. In the older child it may be better to let him pray silently, although if possible get him to ask for forgiveness orally.

A few additional words will help to strengthen him for the future. Turn to John 10:28. Always use your Bible instead of quoting the verses. Let the child read the verses himself when you are dealing with him. If he cannot read, turn to the verse, point to it, and tell him that is what God says. This is much more effective than when the child only hears the verse quoted.

With the child looking at John 10:28, "And I give unto them eternal life; and they shall never perish, neither shall any man pluck them out of my hand," ask him where he is now. Help him with the verse until he says, "In Jesus' hand." Hold out one hand, cupped.

"Yes, Jesus holds you in His hand." Now read the next verse. "Whose hand does it say you are in? Who is the Father? It is as if the Father took His hand (take other hand, place it over cupped hand), "and put it over Jesus' hand, and said, 'You are safe, no one can get you now.' " Show him from this that he does not need to be saved again, but rather to confess his sins.

"You may be unhappy in their hands, but you do not need to be saved again. The way to be happy is to do as they tell us in the Bible, but if you forget and sin, then tell God about it right away and He will forgive you. One way to stay happy is to tell others that you are saved." Read Psalm 107:2: "Let the redeemed of the Lord say so, whom he hath redeemed from the hand of the enemy."

"Whose hand were you in before? Who is the enemy?" This little study about the hands may be used with even a very small child to illustrate this truth.

Again we state the reasons why a child responds to the invitation more than once:

1. He may desire to repeat a happy experience.
2. He may not be saved.
3. He may not have the assurance of his salvation.
4. He may be out of fellowship because of sin.

There is a reason why the child comes forward or raises his hand repeatedly. Do not dismiss him without help. Find out the reason and deal with him accordingly.

2

MAKING MEMORY WORK INTERESTING

In this changing world we need something to which we may cling, something which is sure and steadfast, something which never changes. Little children are caught in the whirl of a swiftly moving age, and may be swept over the edge of some dangerous precipice unless they have something constant in their lives. What could be better than the sure Word of God, the Word which is "settled in heaven," that Word which shall never pass away. It will help them in their youth to remember their Creator, and will in their old age point them to a loving Father who cares for them. It will never be wasted, for it will be brought to mind by the ever-present Holy Spirit, who makes the Son of God real to us. What a great privilege belongs to the teacher of little children; she is in partnership with the Trinity. God gave the Word, Jesus is the Word, and the Holy Spirit reveals the Word. Surely there is no greater honor than to endow a spiritually poverty-stricken child with precious nuggets of God's Word which shall never grow dim.

Not only is the child enriched, he becomes enthusiastic about learning Scripture passages. It is a challenge to him, and engages all the powers of the

most brilliant members of the class who are sometimes apt to lose interest and cause trouble. Little
Richard was a child whose powers needed to be
engaged, or the result would be that some other child
about to sit down would find himself on the floor
instead of in his seat. He was always disrupting the
class, until a new memory work contest was started
and stars were awarded for each verse learned, with
a New Testament as an award when the course was
completed. He was tremendously interested from the
very first. But since he was only eight, and since his
grandmother with whom he lived was blind, we
thought that he would not be able to do a great deal
of memory work. The next Sunday we were surprised. He had learned twenty verses perfectly! After
that we never had any trouble with discipline.
Richard was intent on earning stars, and was too
busy to be naughty. Memory work presents a challenge to the child.

Very often children feel that it is impossible for
them to learn Bible verses. One teacher appealed to
the spiritual side of the saved children. She showed
them the great value of having God's Word hidden
in their hearts. She then told them that Jesus had
promised "whatsoever ye shall ask in my name, that
will I do." "Now, children, whenever a task con-
fronts you that is too hard for you to do by yourself,
just ask God in Jesus' name to help you, and He has
promised that He will." She gave to each child
memory sheets which had ten verses to be memorized,
with the Gospel of John as an award for learning
them.

After the class was over a little girl just seven
whose mother had visited the class said to her mother,

"Oh, mother, I don't know what to do. This nice teacher expects us to learn these verses, and I can't. I just know I can't. What will I do next week at the Bible Club when she asks me and I haven't learned them?"

"Why don't you do what the teacher said? Ask Jesus to help you."

Little Mary took the memory sheet, went into her bedroom, shut the door, and was quiet for two hours. When she came out she ran to her mother. "Oh, mother, Jesus did help me. Just think I have learned five whole verses, and I didn't think I could learn any."

If you appeal to the spiritual side of the child it will help him to put into practice what he learns in the story time.

Many teachers believe in teaching the children verses from God's Word, but have been unable to make it interesting, and for this reason have given it up. It is for those who wish to make memory work attractive to children that this chapter is written. There are many ways to teach Scripture verses which appeal to the boys and girls to such an extent that they will love to memorize and to repeat God's Word.

TEACHING THE VERSE

As it is much easier to learn something with which we are familiar than something absolutely strange, it is well to acquaint the children with the verses even before they attempt to learn them. The teacher may quote them in telling the Bible story to bring out a salient point, she may use them in connection with a song or with another verse. If she is familiar with the verses which are to be taught in the future she can without much effort find many places to use them. Unconsciously the boys and girls will be a little more familiar with the memory work when they come to learn it. That excellent Bible game, the Sword Drill, lends itself to this in a remarkable manner. As it consists of looking up verses in the Bible, the teacher merely chooses those verses which are to be memorized. This drill may also be used to teach the books of the Bible. You will find that the children will enter into it with glee, and care will have to be taken that they do not become too hilarious.

The Sword Drill

Introduce it to the children in a way similar to the following: "Today we are having a war. In wars different weapons are used. I am thinking of a weapon which was used in wars a long time ago. Can anyone think of what it might be?" Let the children guess, but give them a hint or two if they do not guess it soon. "When men fought with swords they had to drill to learn how, just as the soldiers drill with their guns now. God has given us a wonderful weapon to use against the worst enemy we have ever known, Satan. It is the 'Sword of the Spirit,' and is sharper than any two-edged sword. It is the Bible." Just as there are two sides in a war, we will have two sides. Those on this side of the room will be the Reds, and the ones over there will be the Blues. I'll write that on the board and will keep score." Later on be sure the sides are evenly divided as to ability. The following orders are given in a military manner before each verse is located.

Attention: Children sit erect.

Sword in Hand: They place Bible on outstretched left hand.

Matthew 4:19: Teacher repeats slowly.

Charge: They look for the verse.

The first one to find the verse stands and reads it. Just to stand first is not to win, but to stand and read the correct verse. (The others may stand after the first one starts to read when they find the verse if the teacher wishes. In case of error, the second child to stand should be given a chance to read the verse. The teacher must watch carefully in order to be absolutely fair. In some cases she may need a helper to watch with her. The following are references to be used in the sword drill on successive days. Suggestions will be given later in the chapter for memorizing the verses. You will notice that some are listed more than once; this will make the children familiar with the words.

First Day	Second Day	Third Day	Fourth Day	Fifth Day
John 10:9	Matt. 4:19	Rom. 3:23	I Cor. 15:4	John 10:30
Matt. 4:19	John 10:9	I Cor. 15:3	John 10:9	John 10:9
John 10:10	John 10:27	John 10:9	John 10:30	Rev. 3:20
Rom. 3:23	Rom. 3:23	Rev. 3:20	Rev. 3:20	John 10:27
Rom. 10:9	Rev. 3:20	John 10:27	John 10:27	Matt. 4:19
John 10:9	John 10:28	Rev. 3:20	Matt. 4:19	I Cor. 15:4
Matt. 4:19	John 10:10	Rom. 10:10	Rom. 10:9	Rev. 3:20
	John 10:29	I Cor. 15:3	I Cor. 15:3	Rom. 10:10
	Rev. 3:20	Rom. 10:9	John 10:28	I Cor. 15:3
	John 3:16	Rom. 3:23	Rom. 10:10	John 10:28
		I Cor. 15:4	John 10:11	John 10:10
		Psalm 51:7	Rev. 3:20	Rom. 10:9
			Matt. 4:19	John 10:30
			John 3:16	Rev. 3:20
				Rom. 3:23
				Psalm 51:7

This drill will not only make the children familiar with many Bible verses, with the use of their Bibles, and provide activity which will fascinate them, but will also add a highlight to any children's program.

As the sword drill serves to introduce the verse without the children's knowledge, so the picture and story serve to introduce it with their knowledge. A picture of the crucifixion for I Corinthians 15:3, 4; Holman Hunt's "The Light of the World" (Christ knocking at the door) for Revelation 3:20; a picture of a shepherd and his sheep or "The Good Shepherd" for John 10:9-11 and John 10:27-30; and a picture of Bible fishermen for Matthew 4:19 will help to indelibly impress the meaning of these verses on the hearts of little children. When a verse is to be taught and no picture is available, a story may be used instead. The alert teacher will collect both pictures and stories against a possible "rainy day."

Teaching with the Blackboard

Colors, always appealing to children, may be employed in chalk to teach the meaning of the verse. God, Jesus, or heaven, may be indicated with gold; eternal life, green; sin, dark brown (to make it visible on black); died or blood, red. The balance of the words are printed in white. The meaning of the verse should always be explained to the child before he attempts to memorize it.

An old method, but an excellent one to teach the verse in class, is to print the verse on the board, tell the children you are going to see if they are smart enough to read something that isn't there. Erase one word at a time and have the children read the verse after each erasure. They are delighted when only one or two words in widely scattered places appear on the board, and they can "read" the whole verse. This way there is some change before each repetition, and the children do not tire of saying the verse repeatedly, which is, of course, necessary for them to learn it. A verse would appear thus in the various stages of "reading" it. For example:

Rom. 3:23   For all have sinned and   short
                       of   glory of God.
Rom. 3:23   all
                                         God.

A child may be chosen to erase the next word, or one child may conduct the whole exercise. The verse is read once by one section of the group, again by the whole group or an individual each time an erasure is made.

Teaching with the Flannelgraph

The same principle may be used with the flannel-graph by printing the verse on cardboard, pasting flannel on the back, and cutting it into separate words. Remove the words one by one as the children read the verse over and over.

Another method with the flannelgraph is to divide the verse into sections and illustrate each section with a picture or drawing. Flannel is pasted on the back of each, and as the verse is repeated by the teacher at the proper place the symbol is placed on the flannel-graph board. The pictures may be made into a book if the board is not available. Always be sure that the reference is included with the pictures. Thus the children look at it each time and it helps them to connect the verse with the reference. Some sugges-tions follow for certain verses. More may be worked out by the teacher herself. Every verse does not lend itself to this treatment.

If pictures cannot be secured, a simple line draw-ing may be made with crayon, black show-card color, or India ink and lettering pen. These may be secured from a stationery store. Each picture should be mounted on flannel, and likewise the reference, which should always be put up first. Each set should be clipped together, for quick use. An alert child may be permitted to place the pictures on the board while he or another child quotes the verse. The children will love to take turns at this—which means that there is lots of repetition and the verse is learned without much effort. After these pictures are pre-pared they may be used again and again, and the teacher herself will find new uses for them. Never throw away a magazine without first removing all the good pictures. Combined with the flannelgraph they make an excellent aid to Scripture memorizing.

Teaching With Motions

Motions, for teaching verses a different way, are given in the following chart. Little children love motions, and they are profitable in memory work as well as in songs. If the teacher always uses the motions when presenting the verse, that thought will be brought to the mind of the child when he sees the corresponding motion. Thus when the child is trying to repeat a verse and gets "stuck," the teacher makes the motion, and he can generally finish the verse. Even an older child may be thus helped through a difficult place, but he need not give the motions at other times if they seem babyish to him.

It is especially helpful in large classes to have the children do their memorizing at home. For this the child should be furnished with the references and the

Verses	Pictures for Flannelgraph	Motions
John 10:9-11	Reference printed	
I am the door:	Door	Point upward
by me if any man enter in,	Man going in door	Hands together close to chest, spread out wide
He shall be saved,	White heart	Finger pointing on each word from left to right
and shall go in and out, and find pasture.	Meadow, or sheep grazing	
The thief cometh not, but for to steal,	A thief, or lion or bear with sheep	Crouching position, hand over eyebrow as if to see if someone is coming
and to kill, and to destroy:		Move finger across throat
I am come that they might have life, and that they might have it more abundantly.	Picture of Christ	Point upward
I am the good shepherd: the good shepherd giveth his life for the sheep.	Picture, "The Good Shepherd" Cross	Point upward
		Arms stretched outward simulating cross
	Sheep	
Matthew 4:19	Reference printed	
And he saith unto them,	A picture of Christ	Point upward
Follow me,		Walk a few steps
and I will make you fishers of men.	Man catching fish	Hands in front as if holding fishing pole

Verses	Pictures for Flannelgraph	Motions
John 10:27-30	Reference printed	
My sheep hear my voice,	Sheep following shepherd, or an ear	Hand to ear
and I know them,		
and they follow me		
And I give unto them eternal life;	Someone giving gift, or an evergreen tree (Explain that as this tree is green when others are dead, so we have life when others do not.)	Move right hand as if to put something in left hand
and they shall never perish,	Flames of fire	Shake head from side to side
neither shall any man pluck them out of my hand.	Cupped hand	Cup hand
My Father, which gave them me, is greater than all; and no man is able to pluck them out of my Father's hand.	Cupped hand	Point hand upward
		Cup hand
		Point upward twice
		Raise left forefinger
I and my Father are one.	A printed figure "1"	
John 3:16	Reference printed	
For God		Point upward
so loved the world,	Picture of globe	Fingers together above head, making circle for "world"
that he gave		Arms stretched outward
his only begotten Son,	Cross	Left finger raised (only one)
	Picture of Christ	
that whosoever	Man, woman, boy, girl	Hands together near chest, stretch out

Verses	Pictures for Flannelgraph	Motions
John 3:16 (Continued) believeth in him		Point upward
should not perish,	Flames of fire	Shake head side to side
but have everlasting life.	Evergreen tree, see John 10.	Point on each word, starting on left
Romans 3:23 For all	Reference printed Boy, girl, man and woman	Hand outstretched, palm down, move from side to side (All under the sun)
have sinned,	Brawl, or boys fighting or girls cheating	Shoulders dropped, hands at one shoulder simulating carrying load
and come short	Ruler	Palms of hands facing each other, signifying "short"
of the glory of God.		Point upward
I Corinthians 15:3, 4 For I delivered unto you first of all	Reference printed A delivery boy	Both hands cupped; move right hand to left hand as if putting something in it on word "delivered"
that which I also received, how that Christ died for our sins according to the scriptures;	Person receiving gift Cross (may be cut from paper) A Bible	Cross Hands together, palms toward face as if reading book
And that he was buried,	Tomb with stone in doorway	Right hand moving downward
and that he rose again	Tomb with stone rolled away	Both hands low, palms up; raise them

Verses	Pictures for Flannelgraph	Motions
I Corinthians 15:3, 4 (Continued) the third day according to the scriptures.	Figure "3" A Bible	Hold up three fingers Hands together as if reading
Revelation 3:20 Behold I stand at the door, and knock: if any man hear my voice, and open the door,	Reference printed A door Hand knocking at door or heart A large door An open door	Hand knocking in air Hand behind ear Right hand over heart, move outward as if opening door Point upward; then to self
I will come in to him, and will sup with him, and he with me.	A set table	Hand to mouth as if drinking from cup
Psalm 51:7 Wash me, and I shall be whiter than snow.	Reference printed Picture of baby in bath Large snowflake	Move hands as if washing Raise hands above head, move fingers up and down and lower hands
Romans 10:9, 10 That if thou shalt confess with thy mouth the Lord Jesus, and shalt believe in thine heart that God hath raised him from the dead, thou shalt be saved.	Reference printed A large mouth Picture of Christ Heart An open tomb A white heart	Point to mouth Point upward Point to heart Both hands low, palms upward Raise them Finger pointing on each word, starting from left to right

verses written out. References are not sufficient as
many do not have Bibles at home. Even if they do,
they will not always go to the trouble of locating
them. We found that fastening the typewritten sheet
to a colored sheet of construction paper greatly reduced the number which were lost. The children
could keep track of something colored more easily
than a white sheet of paper. A couple of staples in
one end, or a bit of yarn may be used to fasten the
pages together. Fold the sheets crosswise and the
child has a booklet. A light colored paper may be
used to write the verses on. A hectograph which
makes duplicate copies in purple ink may be secured
reasonably from a mail order house or stationery
store, and will materially lessen the work of making
the copies for each child. It is not necessary to have
a typewriter to use these. Always make some extra
ones as some will be lost. When the memory work
is done at home, the verse may be recited to someone
at a table at the entrance. This gives individual attention to all but does not take valuable class time. A
child should never be given credit for a verse until
he can recite it perfectly with the reference. For the
little children a rule that they must say the verse
twice perfectly helps them to overlearn it before trying to say it.

One thing we can never get away from in the
learning process is repetition. It takes unfailing patience to urge a child to say again and again a simple
verse. We must realize that two or three times will
not suffice, but that it must be over and over again.
Before the meeting begins, or after it is over, the
teacher can often help the child who has difficulty.
In fact it is a good idea for the teacher to consider

herself occupied for fifteen minutes before the opening time, and fifteen minutes after the time for
closing. Those few minutes can be very profitable, and
some child who is too backward to try in class will
be persuaded to attempt learning a verse when a
loving teacher is giving all her attention to him.

While the teacher must be loving she must also be
fair, and not wink at mistakes and award the child
who stumbles through a verse equally with one who
has said it perfectly. Maintain a high standard. Insist
that a verse be repeated correctly with no help from
you before it is counted. I know it is hard to do this.
Some little child not quite so brilliant as the others
has forgotten to learn his verse at home and hearing
the others say it several times he can get through it,
if you help him three or four times. Should this verse
be counted as memorized? Absolutely not. Do not
discourage the child, but help him individually all you
can. If he cannot say it at the close of the time
allotted, encourage him to come back the next time
and earn his star then.

If a child tries to say a verse and almost succeeds,
he should be encouraged, helped by the teacher, or an
older child, until he can say it, but should not be
given credit until he has come up to the standard.
At first, children will try to slip by with shoddy
memory work, but if a high standard is maintained,
they will learn their verses more carefully.

One class increased its attendance by having each
child teach the memory verse to some other child
who was not present. The one who taught the verse
received extra training on it; the other child became
interested in the class through the memory work.
When a list of verses is being memorized as in a

contest, the child may be given a star each time he says a verse, and then required to review that verse on a different day, which accomplishment is indicated by a check mark after the star. Then, at the close the verses should all be said at one time. By making individual charts for each child and posting them on the bulletin board only after the child has earned two stars, real interest can be awakened and maintained.

NAME OF CHILD		
	Stars	Check Mark
Romans 3:23	*	√
Romans 10:9, 10 (2 stars)	**	√
Revelation 3:20	*	
I Corinthians 15:3, 4 (2 stars)		
John 10:9-11 (3 stars)		
John 10:27-30 (4 stars)		
Matthew 4:19		
John 3:16		
Psalm 51:7		

The child whose chart is given above had recited the first three passages, and had reviewed the first two. The stars or check marks should be given immediately after the child recites the verse. Psychologists tell us that this attaches a satisfying reaction to the effort of learning the verse. The next time he will be ready and willing to learn. In one class the teacher strung symbols on ribbon immediately after the child said a verse, with 100% results. In another class the same teacher used the same symbols, and same verses, but strung them after class. Although the children saw their memory strings the following week the percentage of verses learned was only 50-75%. The immediate reward is most effective.

The following system may be used as a guide in memory work.

Number of verses	Award
one verse	one silver star
ten silver stars	one gold star
two gold stars	Bible story book
five gold stars	New Testament

A Gospel of John may be awarded when the first gold star is earned. The teacher will find that a ceremony making a special occasion of the giving of the awards will add greatly to the zeal of the children in future memory work. The room may be arranged in a specially attractive way. Teacher might wear her prettiest dress, and the children earning awards could sit in special seats. The teacher could give a little speech before presenting the awards. Even if it be something very inexpensive, homemade, or costing one cent, the value of it to the child is enhanced immeasurably by the ceremony that accompanies it. Remember it is not the money you spend on awards that counts, it is the value that you endue them with in the mind of the pupil that matters. Do not spoil your children by starting out with expensive awards. Pick something that a child will like, even if it costs only a few cents. I still recall the pleasure we as children received from a ten cent top one Christmas, while expensive presents went unheeded. It is not the amount of money spent that counts.

Once during a memory contest select several of the children who have done especially good work, and ask them to tell how they memorized their verses. Some will say they learn their verses right after school, some just before they go to bed, and others will have an unusual method of memorizing. Such a service will encourage the others to go on with their work with greater vigor.

REVIEWING MEMORY WORK

Reviewing is just as important as memorizing. The verses should become so fixed in the mind and heart of the child that they will never be forgotten, and there are many excellent methods to accomplish this end. Remember that each time a verse is said in your class it will help to fix it in the minds of the children. The problem is to see that the verses are said many times and yet maintain interest. The devices suggested will help.

Flannelgraph Ships

By use of the flannelgraph an interesting way of review for primaries may be devised. Find in a magazine or make two ships identical except for color. Paste flannel on the back. Make two identical sets of big waves which may be strips of blue flannel about four inches wide, reaching clear across the flannelgraph. Cut waves with scissors. Divide the class in two groups. First one side, then the other, is given an opportunity to say the verse. Each successful attempt causes the ship to move forward one wave.

After each unsuccessful one, it moves backward. The children's desire is to get their ship across the board first. Yours is to get them to repeat the same verse correctly many times without tiring of it.

For variety, on another day use airplanes with varying heights in altitude; or autos with miles marked, bicycles with city blocks, or train engines with different cities designated.

The Popcorn Drill

When the children know as many as three verses you may begin to use this drill, which they dearly love. The drill might be introduced as follows:

"How many of you have ever watched your mothers pop corn? Of course you have. Just what happens when she does it? First, she puts some grains of corn in a kettle, then she turns on the fire; and then what happens? Pretty soon, we hear, 'Pop, pop, pop, pop' almost faster than you can count. Now we are going to have a popcorn drill. Each one of you will be a grain of popcorn. When I say 'Ready' that will be turning on the fire; and you will 'pop' by standing and saying a verse of Scripture. If someone says the verse that you know, just say it anyway. Grains of popcorn are often alike. What is in the bottom of the pan after your mother is through popping the corn? Yes, some grains that didn't pop. There will be some here who will not 'pop.' They are just like those grains. I hope you aren't like them."

This drill may be used for a short period each meeting, and will furnish a good review of previous memory work.

8 to 12 years

Puzzles

An activity which is useful in reviewing memory work for the early-comers is found in puzzles. On strips of cardboard print the reference and words of the memory passage in letters ½ or ¾ of an inch high. Use different colored crayon, or show-card color for each passage to facilitate assembling if they should become mixed. Then cut between each word, and the child can have the job of putting them in the proper order on a table or on the flannelgraph if flannel is used on the reverse side of the cards. If two sets are available on the same verse, the children love to race to see which one can finish first. Boys and girls from eight to twelve are in the puzzle age. Why not use that for the Lord? One youngster wanted me to make a puzzle of the whole twenty-third Psalm, but I drew the line at that. Perhaps I should have had more patience. A sample of a puzzle follows:

Romans 3:23	For	all	have	sinned	and
come	short	of	the	glory	of	God.

The longer passages may include several words in one piece, and the children be permitted to use their Bibles. Later the Bible is excluded, and the cardboard cut into a piece for each word.

Riddles

Children of Junior age like riddles as well as puzzles. Verses may suggest simple ones. To guess, the child must state the reference and quote the entire verse before told whether or not he has chosen the right verse. The group may enter in as a whole, or may be divided into sides, and points given for each one correctly guessed. Remember each time a verse is repeated it is traced deeper on the heart and mind of the child. Our job is to make that repeating interesting. Given below are samples. Make up your own. It isn't hard.

Rom. 3:23 I am thinking of a verse that tells something about everyone in the whole world. It isn't about their hair, or about their eyes, and it isn't very nice. What verse is it?

I Cor. 15:3, 4 I am thinking of a verse that starts with something sad, and ends with something glad. The glad part happened three days after the sad part.

Rev. 3:20 I am thinking of a door, and Someone is making a noise at the door. What verse does that remind you of?

Rom. 10:9, 10 I am thinking of a verse which says something about a mouth, and a heart, and tells how to be saved.

John 10:9-11 What is the place where cows are driven to each morning? What is a person who steals? And who is the person who takes care of animals, but not cows? The right answer to each question is a word in each one of the three verses in this passage.

John 10:27-30 I am thinking of a soft little animal, and a part of our body with which we hold things. What verses does this tell about?

John 3:16 I am thinking of Someone who had something He loved very much. He had only one, and yet He gave it.

Psalm 51:7 I am thinking of something cold and white which we generally see in winter.

What Verse Could You Tell

This exercise is similar to riddles, but is more on the thought of the verse, and gives good training for personal work. Primary children as a rule are too young for this, but it is excellent training for the Junior and Intermediate child. The procedure is the same as for riddles, the child repeating the reference and whole verse before being told whether or not he is right. Frequently, the child will quote a verse which would apply perfectly, but was not the one you had in mind. Of course, he should be given credit.

Rom. 3:23 One day a boy tells you he has never done anything wrong. What verse in the Bible could you tell him to show that is not true?

I Cor. 15:3 A girl tells you that Jesus was just a good man, and that He never did anything for her. What verse could you tell to show her He did do something for her?

Rev. 3:20 Someone tells you that it is very, very hard to get Jesus to come into your heart. They say that you have to be very good, go to church all the time, do lots and lots of good things, and still maybe Jesus won't come into your heart. What verse could you tell which says that it is easy to get Jesus to come into your heart?

Rom. 10:9, 10 A boy says that it is all right to believe in Jesus, but you never need to say anything about it with your mouth. What verse could you tell?

John 10:9-11 Someone says there are lots of ways to heaven, and lots of good leaders. If we just follow one we shall be saved and shall have life abundantly. What verse could you tell?

John 10:27-30 A boy asks you, "If I would put myself in Jesus' hand could anyone ever take me out of it?" What verse could you tell?

John 3:16 Someone says, "I don't believe God has a Son." What verse could you tell?

Psalm 51:7 Someone says, "I don't believe your sins can be washed away so that you are really clean." What verse could you tell?

Games

A party for children may be enlivened with games which use memory verses as a background. Pin on the wall pictures which go with the memory verse. Number each picture. Give each contestant a list of the references and have him put the number of the correct picture opposite the reference. Score the individuals or divide group into sides. Bibles should be available for visitors. Of course, one who knows the verses has a distinct advantage but the others will not feel left out.

For a relay race print the verses on one sheet of paper in large letters, and on another sheet print the reference. Make two sets. Line the children up as for a relay race some distance away from a table where the verses are spread out in clear view. At the signal the first one in each line runs to the table, picks up the top reference, chooses the verse to go with it, and hands it to one of two adults. If it is correct, he takes the next reference to the next child in line. If it is incorrect, he must look up the reference in the Bible, and thus choose the correct one. The adult may post the reference and verse together on a bulletin board after they are handed her, for the remaining children in line to study. Several copies of the verses and references which are difficult for the children to associate may be made, and the very repetition will help the children to remember them.

Use a blackboard to print scrambled verses, the letters of the words being mixed up. With pencil and paper the children may unscramble them. A sample follows:

LLA AVEH NNESID NAD MECO HRTSO FO HET LOYGR FO ODG Answer: Rom. 3:23.

For variety, the words, instead of letters, might be mixed. One twelve-year-old boy liked this so much that he stayed after class during the time for his favorite radio program, to finish a whole list of scrambled verses.

These helps to learning memory work have all been tried and found to work. But in speaking to teacher training classes the author has found that the teachers do not always try them, thinking that these things would not appeal to their children. All we ask is that you try and see. Perhaps you also, like some who tried them after great insistence, will be amazed at the interest and enthusiasm for God's Word that they will arouse.

3

TEACHING THE CHILD TO PRAY

STRETCHED out before the teacher is the "beautiful garden of prayer"—a sunny, eastern slope with lofty heights and many lovely nooks and dells. In her hand is placed that of another, not a full grown man who has seen it all before, but a tiny toddler, a precious little child. It is her glorious privilege to introduce this place of wonder and beauty to the child. She will not expect her little charge to exhaust its wonder in a day—ah no, they will make many trips before even a part of this garden is traversed. For the child is very small, and he has never been this way before. Besides, his little legs are weak, and as she would use patience and love in teaching him to walk physically, she uses just as much patience in acquainting him with this beautiful garden. No matter what his actual age, spiritually he is just a new-born child of God. She will not be discouraged if he can only take a step or two at first. She will not give up if he forgets just where that beautiful flower grew that she showed him the day before; but over and over again she will show him some small thing, then lead him a bit farther day after day, until soon he has grown to love the garden, and can come to it even when she is not with him.

The entrance to the garden is the gate of salvation. Only the redeemed ones, born-again children of

Father God are permitted inside. She does not make
the mistake of trying to show the garden of prayer
from the outside through this gate. The child, being
so small, could not see over the wall, and soon it
would grow very dull to him, even if he should pre-
tend to walk its paths. But once he has entered
through faith in Christ Jesus, even though he gets
only a little glimpse, he wants to come again and
each time the garden grows more precious to him.

THE FIRST PRAYER

Ideally, the child makes his first prayer as he
enters the gate to the garden. That is when he accepts
Christ as his personal Saviour. God's Word says that
the way into the holiest, the very presence of God,
is through the blood of Jesus. "Having therefore,
brethren, boldness to enter into the holiest by the
blood of Jesus, By a new and living way, which he
hath consecrated for us, through the veil, that is to
say, his flesh" (Heb. 10:19, 20). The mere repetition
of words is not prayer. Reciting by rote does not
necessarily gain the audience of God. True prayer
is coming into His presence through the blood of His
only Son; audible words may or may not be used.
So in teaching our little ones, let us bring them by
the right way unto Him in prayer. It is so easy to
teach them correctly in the first place, but much
more difficult to train them after they have been
instructed erroneously. Let us remember that this
discussion concerns the child in the meeting, not the
child in the home. For by the time he is old enough
to come to meetings, he is generally old enough to be
brought to the Saviour. Thus the child's first prayer,

through which he enters into the beautiful garden, is that one in which he receives Jesus Christ as his own Saviour.

This prayer is not difficult, and should not fill the worker with apprehension, for it is merely talking to God and asking for His salvation. The teacher makes the children understand what it is. The word "pray" or "prayer" may not even be mentioned. For the average child a mysterious something with which he is not familiar is brought to mind along with this vocabulary. Of course, these words are introduced as time goes on, but we must take care not to frighten the child or he will be afraid to take this first step. Other suggestions are given in the chapter "Inviting the Child to Christ."

If you had never seen a group at prayer, would not the sudden bowing of heads, and closing of eyes arouse your curiosity? Be one jump ahead of the child who is always curious. Tell him in advance what is going to happen, and then he will not be curious. "When we talk to Jesus, we bow our heads (teacher bows her head), and close our eyes (teacher closes her eyes), and think about Jesus, for it is to Him we are talking." Then the teacher has the boys and girls follow her example. If these instructions are given every time before prayer with the smaller children, they will soon learn to have a quiet, reverent attitude. Some would ask, should we have the children kneel? The answer is to lead the child a step at a time. If you try several, he may stumble. One group of children were earnestly listening as their teacher explained salvation. She had them kneel, and the experience was so new and different that they became occupied with it, and started to giggle. It was only with difficulty that she recaptured their attention. It might have been wiser to have waited to teach them this physical position for prayer.

THE PRAYER OF THANKSGIVING

The entrance to the garden is so close to the flower of thankfulness that the second prayer may follow close on the heels of the first. The child's thoughts are already centered on what Christ has done for him, thus it requires little effort to get him to say "thank you" to the Saviour. This is a flower that the little child loves to visit. Somehow it seems that it does not appear so lovely to the older ones. I have seen a group of twenty Primary and Beginner children drill with eagerness as they were asked, "Who would like to thank Jesus because He died on the Cross for us?" Twenty little hands would go up, and no one was satisfied until all twenty little hearts had thanked their dear Saviour. It was not just once, but time after time these dear little tots stopped before the flower of thankfulness and enjoyed its beauty one after the other. Cannot we adults, so eager to get to the place of petition, learn a lesson from these little ones?

> Oh, that men would praise the Lord for his good-
> ness, and for his wonderful works to the children of
> men! (Psalm 107:31)

Yes, we have His goodness in the sunshine, our parents, our food, and in various physical blessings, but we must not forget to teach the child to thank Him because we are His children, because He has forgiven our sins, because He is going to take us to heaven, and because He answers our prayers. Remembering our "step at a time" rule, mention only one of these at a time, or if you wish, mention several, and let each child choose with you before prayer time the one for which he wishes to thank the Lord. Children do not understand a "season of prayer," therefore we go around the entire group in an orderly manner mentioning the child's name before that one prays, or having the child who wishes to pray next, raise his hand.

THE EMERGENCY PRAYER

After the prayer of thanksgiving, teach the child the emergency prayer—that short prayer in which the heart is lifted to God in time of need. The prayer of sinking Peter is an example of this. The hard place in which the Israelites found themselves as they faced the Red Sea was depicted to one class of children. "There was a mountain to the left, a mountain to the right, the sea in front, and behind them came the onrushing Egyptians. They did not know what to do. They were in a hard place. The Bible says they cried unto the Lord. That means, children, that they prayed. The Lord rolled the waters back and made a dry path right through the Red Sea. They were safe from the Egyptians. Now, this next week some of you children may be in a hard place—we cannot tell. If you are, will you remember to ask the Lord to help you? Next week we will ask you to tell about the hard place that you were in and how the Lord helped you."

In one class the following week little Ralph, a freckled-faced red-haired mischief of eight spoke up. "Well, I was in a hard place. Our neighbors lost their dog, Shep, and they called and called him, and he didn't come. He was a good dog, too. I hunted and hunted for him, but I couldn't find him. Finally I thought, 'Why, this is a hard place, I'll ask Jesus to help me.' And so I did. Then I went right over a little hill, and there was Shep. Jesus really helped me." Now that child has experienced a definite answer to prayer, and it will not be so difficult for him to voice an audible prayer. Little Dorothy reported, "I was in a hard place, too. My tooth was loose, and Daddy wanted to pull it, but I was afraid. I asked Jesus to help me, so I wouldn't be afraid, and He did. Then I let my Daddy pull it, and it didn't even hurt."

It is the desire of the Lord not only to have these boys and girls, but to enter into every part of their lives. The pulling of a tooth, or the finding of a lost dog is very real to a little child, and if he finds the Lord sufficient for these things, he will trust the Lord as he grows older.

PRIVATE PRAYER

Coming to the "garden of prayer" with the teacher is precious, but coming all alone is infinitely sweeter. A fragrance comes from the lives of those who have this habit which others do not know. Even a child is not too young to form the habit of coming regularly to the Lord in prayer. What power there would be in our churches today if all the members were accustomed to spend time alone with God every day.

There is no better story to introduce this new step than the age-old one of Daniel. Daniel, who prayed regularly. Daniel, who was not afraid of the officers who sought his downfall. Daniel, who would rather pray and be thrown to the lions, than not to pray. What an example of courage and bravery! What a hero to present to young worshippers! And then to bring home the story. "Will you pray every day? No one will throw you to the lions, but someone might make fun of you. Will you be brave enough to stand against that and still pray? Or will you be a coward, and quit? Or will you say, 'I'm too tired tonight.' That's not being brave. I hope everyone in our class will be as brave as Daniel was."

In seeking to develop regular devotional habits in the believing child it is well to employ a prayer chart. The teacher may make these previously, or the children may make them in a handwork period. Use colored construction paper as the base. Paste at the top a picture suggestive of prayer, such as Daniel in the lions' den, Christ in Gethsemane, or the boy Samuel at prayer. Rule a piece of white paper to resemble a calendar, but omit the numerals. List the days of the week at the top of this white sheet over the proper squares. Punch two holes in the top of the construction paper, and use yarn or colored string through them so that the chart will hang on the child's bedroom wall. Each night the child marks "P" in the proper square if he prayed that day. He draws a circle around the "P" if he read the Bible. Although this is a very simple device, the teacher will be surprised at the interest it will arouse in regular prayer and Bible reading. The chart serves as an ever-present reminder against the old excuse, "I forgot."

Gordon was only eight years old, but he had made a prayer chart in Sunday school. His mother said to the teacher, "It doesn't make any difference how late it is, or in how much of a hurry I am, Gordon simply will not go to bed until he has read the Bible and prayed."

The little books, "Daily Bread," by Ruth P. Overholtzer, are ideal to use in a planned devotional program for children. Each book contains an appealing reading for each day in a month, with suitable stories and poems illustrating Bible verses, especially for children. Of course, nothing takes the place of the Bible.

The private devotional life of a Christian is the basis for his growth. Therefore, let us do everything in our power to firmly establish this habit in the lives of our saved children in order that they will stand true to the Lord in spite of trials and temptations.

PUBLIC PRAYER

If the suggestions already given have been followed, the child has prayed publicly upon receiving Christ as his Saviour, he has prayed again publicly thanking Jesus for saving him, he has turned to the Lord in time of emergency, and has prayed by himself at home. By now he is more or less familiar with the mechanics of prayer, a foundation has been established, and the child is ready to proceed. It may take a period of several weeks to arrive at this point if there is only one contact a week with the child. But do not make the mistake of trying to build without this foundation, for it simply will not stand. In seeking to lead children in prayer it is better to make the step that you ask them to take so small that you are reasonably sure that they will respond in the way you desire, rather than making such a big step that the children would be afraid to try. This truth cannot be overemphasized. Do not expect too much at once, but have your goal in mind and proceed that way slowly, but very definitely. I believe that there is no great truth of the Bible or of the Christian life that cannot be taught to children if this is kept in mind. Review is implied here to a great extent. God said, "For precept must be upon precept, precept upon precept; line upon line, line upon line; here a little, and there a little" (Isa. 28:10).

In having public prayer in a class there should be some definite reason for it. A classmate who is ill, a child's father who needs work, and friends and relatives who are not saved, are all suitable subjects for prayer. At first it might be well to have one request and let several who desire pray about it. Later on the children themselves may bring the requests and the teacher appoint or let different children take certain requests to the Lord in prayer. Remember that this is the children's prayer time, and only those things that are real to the children should be prayed about. If the teacher desires that the children pray for some missionary friend, this person and the field should first be made real to the children by means of letters, pictures, stories, etc. Children generally do pray in faith, and we have available a great power for God if we would train our saved children to pray for the Lord's work. It must also be remembered that adult prayers before children should be suitable. Paul says that we are to pray "with the understanding," but how can this be if the adult prays with a vocabulary foreign to the understanding of the child. These prayers should be simple and short. As the children grow in grace the prayers may be a trifle longer, but as a rule they should be kept short. If you have some-one visit your class who is known for his long-winded praying do not honor him by asking him to lead in prayer. It will throw cold water on the child's in-terest. Honor him some other way. As the children grow in grace even prayers usually voiced by an adult may be entrusted to a child. Think what agony these children will be spared if when older someone calls suddenly upon them to lead in prayer.

THE MEALTIME PRAYER

The story of Jesus feeding the five thousand is an example to give to the children in establishing the practice of thanking the Lord for our food. Possibly many children come from homes where this Christian practice is not observed, but where the parents would not be antagonistic if their pride and joy were to make the suggestion that he thank God for the food. Besides establishing the children, this gives a definite testimony to parents who need it. Make the sugges-tion to the older children when they are no longer afraid to pray publicly, and at the next meeting in-quire as to what success they had. The younger chil-dren might pray with the teacher through the day's meals after the class is over. They could mention what they had on the table for breakfast, and one child could thank the Lord. Enough meals could thus be pretended to give each child a chance to return thanks. No one knows the effect these simple prayers will have carried to unbelieving parents.

Sometimes for variety the following verses may be used as mealtime prayers. The second goes with the melody of the Doxology.

> God is great and God is good,
> And we thank Him for our food,
> By His goodness all are fed,
> Give us Lord our daily bread.

> We thank thee Lord for this our food,
> For life and health and every good.
> Let manna to our souls be given,
> The Bread of life sent down from heaven.

ELEMENTS IN PRAYER

We have discussed the occasions for prayer, but a few words on the elements of prayer might be suitable. Worship, thanksgiving, petition, confession, and communion are all elements of prayer. Most of these have been mentioned, but one or two need further developing.

Worship

The spirit of worship is necessary to true prayer. Too many children's meetings are of the "hip, hip, hurrah" variety, with no thought given to true worship. The leaders should be enthusiastic, and keep the interests of children in mind, but each meeting should have a time of quiet worship. One way which was most helpful in fostering this spirit in several groups was the use of the prayer chorus. Public prayer was held at a regular time in each meeting, but before the prayer, heads were bowed, eyes closed, while the piano softly accompanied muted voices singing a quiet chorus. Then the room was still while all the hearts listened when one or several led the group to

the throne of grace. There was no hush-hushing of
the group to get them quiet enough for a hurried
prayer. The chorus had brought about a reverent
spirit of worship. There are many such choruses.
Search through your chorus books for one appropriate to your group. Use this chorus only before
your prayer, not at any other time, except while
learning it. Always sing it softly and reverently, and
you will find a true spirit of worship will prevail in
your prayer time. One we used with great effect is
to the tune of "Into My Heart." The author of the
words is not known.

sing

> Out of my life, out of my life,
> Shine out of my life, Lord Jesus;
> Shine out today, Shine out alway,
> Shine out of my life, Lord Jesus.

Thanksgiving and Petition

For a discussion on the second element of prayer,
see "The Prayer of Thanksgiving" at the beginning
of this chapter. Petition is also discussed under "The
Emergency Prayer" and "Public Prayer." In addition, the children should be taught to ask in Jesus'
name, John 14:13, 14; in faith, Mark 11:24; recog-
nizing the Father's will, I John 5:14, 15; making
definite requests, John 14:14. To encourage them in
faith, tell them of your own answers to prayer, and
the answers that other children have had. Encourage
them to tell in class when God answers prayer for
them.

Confession of Sin

Just as we need to teach the child to thank the
Lord and ask Him for his needs, so we also must
teach him to confess his sins to the Heavenly Father.

I John 1:9: If we confess our sins, he is faithful and just
        to forgive us our sins, and to cleanse us from
        all unrighteousness.

During a junior girls' handicraft class several girls
seemed to be quarreling. As the days went by their
spirit became worse, and different ones began to
tattle to the teacher. None of the tales agreed, but
knowing that these girls had publicly accepted Christ,
the teacher knew that this spirit of anger and bitterness should not exist. Each one tried to tell her side,
and the bickering almost spoiled the class. Finally the
teacher drew each of the four girls into an adjoining
room, and handed each a Bible. "Now, I don't want
to hear each one of the sides of this quarrel. That
would not do any good at all. But I want us to see
what God has to say. Let us turn to Ephesians 4:31,
32. Mary, you read it to us.

"Let all bitterness, and wrath, and anger, and clamour,
and evil speaking, be put away from you, with all malice:
And be ye kind one to another, tenderhearted, forgiving one
another, even as God for Christ's sake hath forgiven you.

"Now the Lord says," went on the teacher, "that
there are five things that He wants put away from
you. Alice, tell us what these five things are." Alice
read the list in the passage.

"I am afraid, girls, that these things have been very
much present in our class. What do you think? Have
you been guilty?" The little heads which had been so
erect as each owner was so sure she was right, began
to droop as the Holy Spirit did His work.

"Now the next verse says that we are to forgive
others even if they do things that are wrong. The
reason is that Christ has paid for their sin. Therefore,
we must not hold it against them. If we do not for-

give, we are disobeying the Lord, and we will be unhappy. How many of you have disobeyed Him?" Four little heads drooped lower as four little hands went up.

Then they all turned to I John 1:9 and the teacher explained that we must not just confess all our sins, but that we must tell the Lord what they are. Each girl admitted that she had sinned, and told the teacher she wanted to ask the Lord to forgive her. A time of prayer followed, with each child taking her guilt to the Lord. After this, those four girls became bosom pals. Instead of quarreling about their handiwork, they were always helping one another. The most ardent disputer confided to the teacher, "Everything is so different now. I'm happy, and those girls are my best friends."

Teachers do not always have such a situation in which to teach confession of sin, but there are many that might unconsciously be passed by. Every time that the truths of the Christian life can be applied to the child in his actual experiences, those truths will be much more real to him than those he learns in theory only.

Through the gate of salvation the teacher has led the child into the "beautiful garden of prayer." It has been a wonderful privilege, for the wonders and glories of this garden are never to be exhausted even if one should spend a lifetime there. It is enough that the teacher should introduce the child to this place and make him sufficiently acquainted with it, so that he will come there by himself; for then the Head Gardener will lead him into paths of communion large enough only for two, so sweet and so precious that they are not seen if another is there.

4

TELLING THE STORY

I love to tell the story,
For some have never heard
The message of salvation
From God's own holy word.

TELLING the gospel story—what a priceless privilege! Angels desire to tell it, but they cannot because they have never been redeemed. No other message is as sweet to the ear as the good news of salvation. Little children who love stories anyway are doubly glad to hear this sweetest of all stories. The story is so precious to God that He has filled His Word with it: a shadow of it here, a suggestion of it there, a golden nugget partly revealed in another passage, until we come into the full glory of the complete revelation given the apostle Paul. All in all, we have a voluminous collection of stories all heading up in one subject, God's beloved Son.

How can we best tell these stories? What will make our storytelling more effective? It is to answer these questions that this chapter is written.

WHAT TO TELL

Is a story with a moral just as good as a Bible story? By no means. "For the word of God is quick, and powerful, and sharper than any twoedged

sword" (Heb. 4:12). Use the Bible story in your
class, and your children will grow in grace and in
the knowledge of the Lord. There is no literature in
the world which surpasses the Bible. Thus in giving
the child the Bible you are giving to him a cultural
background as well as a spiritual foundation. In cases
where the children meet more than once a week, or
for a lengthy period of time, a missionary story may
be included for variety, but even this should not take
the place of the Bible story. Other incidents may be
used as illustrations within the story, but first and
foremost is the story from God's own Word. A series
of stories with a central theme is generally best to
follow.

One person starting to teach children for the first
time said, "I'm just going to teach out of my head
and tell them all I know." This is a mistake, for those
who have had experience have points of value to pass
on to those who follow. If one ever did try to get
along without the helps, it should be only after years
of experience in teaching children the Word of God.

Preparing to tell the story is almost as important
as the actual telling, for the results depend largely
on this factor. Last minute study, no matter how
intensive, is never as favorable to good storytelling
as that which takes place over a period of time. The
mind and heart need time to think and to meditate,
during which the Holy Spirit has opportunity to
speak to the teacher. Several weeks beforehand read
a few of the stories you are to tell, and at least a
week before telling a particular story start your
preparation. In this way the story will be thoroughly
mastered by the time it is to be told. The details are

not hazy in the mind, and new points of spiritual truth are discovered each time the story is read.

The teacher's preparation is not complete until she knows the story thoroughly. Reading it in the Bible comes first, then the helps follow. Some people find help in making a brief outline of the story, and by putting down on paper the main points, they master the trend of the story. But the preparation is not all intellectual, it includes the heart as well. If the story means something to the teacher it will mean something to the children. A great Bible teacher once said, "If we speak out of our heads the message will enter into the heads of our listeners, but if we speak out of our hearts, it will enter into their hearts." Conduct is changed because of a change of heart. Therefore since we wish to influence the heart, we must see that our own heart is warmed by the story. A very conscientious teacher said, "Telling the story is so much easier for me now. I used to study so carefully, attend a teacher training class, and then try to tell the story exactly as it was told there. One day the leader told us that the Holy Spirit desired to use us in the telling of the story, and that we should depend upon Him. Now I still study carefully, and I still attend the teacher training class, but instead of trying so hard in my own strength, I turn it over to the Lord, and He brings new light on the story as I go about my housework. It is much easier now. I tried hard before, but now He just seems to do it."

For those who have not had much experience, practice is almost imperative. One young man got his start as a minister by preaching to the cabbage heads on his father's farm. The teacher of little children may practice on her own children, those of a neighbor, or even on the breakfast dishes. Many are just afraid of the sound of their own voices, and this oral practice aids in attaining poise before a group. The teacher will be more than repaid for the effort involved in getting adequate preparation.

HOW TO TELL IT

With Forcefulness

If the story has forcefulness and expression, it is really a good one. To make her story forceful, the teacher should first of all have a purpose in telling it. She is not just telling a story, she has a point that she wants to put across, something she wishes to accomplish in the lives of the children. At first this great aim should be to lead the children to Christ, but later on it may include leading them into closer fellowship with Christ, causing them to desire to yield their lives to Him for service, or making them want to give their testimony at every opportunity. The story is a means to an end, and not the end itself.

After the aim has been decided upon, the teacher should build to a climax. It is as if she were building a children's slide. Each point is another step in the ladder, with the climax at the peak where the slide starts. In building a slide, even if one had a very attractive piece of lumber, if it were not long enough for a step he would not use it. It is the same way in a story. No matter how good a point is, if it does not fit, do not use it. Eliminate all extraneous material. In telling a story, the things you leave out are just as important as the things you include. Every sentence should bring you one step nearer the climax.

A little suspense goes a long way in making an interesting story. Don't give the ending to your story too soon. In telling of Daniel and the lions, don't say at the beginning of the story, "But the lions didn't get him." That is to throw away your suspense. Keep the children sitting on the anxious seat wondering what will happen next.

With Expression *very good instruction*

Everyone loves a story that is well told. Putting expression into the words, the voice, and the body aids considerably in making a well-told tale.

Use words that give a vivid picture of the scene, by giving the specific details. In telling of David, either of the following statements might be used, but the latter is more graphic, because the specific details are given. We get a clearer picture of what actually happened. "An animal came from behind something and attacked a sheep." "A lion sprang from behind the bushes, and sank his teeth into the throat of a sheep."

Comparison often makes clear to little children those things which are outside their experience. Some city children have never seen thorns, yet if it is explained that they are sharp like needles, but grow on bushes, the story of the crucifixion will be more real to them. The thorns which were outside of the realm of their knowledge were compared to needles which were familiar to them. Comparison is of great value in linking the known to the unknown. Use it freely in Bible stories, for it will aid in greater comprehension. Like comparison, contrast clears up the meaning. Instead of telling what points are similar, it shows the places of difference.

In telling of the two thieves, the teacher could say, pointing to the crosses drawn on the board or displayed on the flannelgraph, "This man, because he accepted Christ, had eternal life, but this man did not. This man was going to paradise, but the other would never get to go because he did not believe in Jesus. The first thief would be with Jesus forever and ever, but the second thief could not be. This man had his sins forgiven, but the other one died without forgiveness." Thus from a Bible story the children get clearly the difference between the saved and the lost. If you want to make your Bible stories live, make the words expressive by using specific detail, comparison, and contrast.

Expression in the voice makes it pleasant to listen to, and consequently the story is more attractive. We have all listened to preachers whose never-changing drone puts the congregation to sleep. It requires much more effort to listen to a monotone than to the voice whose pitch is first high, and then low. A monotone is like listening to one note on the piano played again and again with no other notes included. The human voice as given by God is capable of great variation. Why employ only one tone when He has given so many? A little practice in conversation by deliberately changing the pitch of the voice will make it easier in telling the story. The same degree of loud-ness may be almost as tiresome as a monotone. Some points are more effective if made in a soft low voice. If you notice the children becoming restless, try either raising or lowering your voice, and very often their attention will be regained. In the same way, speak slowly part of the time, and quickly at other times. To give the impression of rapid action speak quickly and use short sentences. Likewise, to convey a peaceful, quiet effect, employ a low voice with long sentences. Change the voice to a high pitch when one character speaks, and to a low tone when the other character answers, and with just this variation the children will see two people carrying on a conversation. Use conversation whenever you can, quoting the words which the character used, or might have used. Direct discourse makes a story vital. Use it whenever possible, taking care to label it as such if imagination is employed. A pleasing voice can adorn the gospel very effectively.

When some people speak before an audience it seems that every part of their body is frozen except their tongue. Yet those same people will show a group of friends how long the fish was, how tall the child was, or how the old man stroked his beard. They use their body to get across their point. We do not need to be actors to tell a good story, but we do need to be natural, and it is natural to use our bodies at least part of the time when we are talking. You may think that you could never move before the children, but if you do it consciously a few times, it will soon become natural, and the children will really enjoy the story more. One small boy watched Miss Frances Bennett, the master storyteller, as she showed how David wound up his sling, and when she made the motion to let the stone go, this little boy ducked. The expression in her body made the story that real to him. For those who would carry this advice of bodily movement too far, a word of warning is given. Never allow your gestures or bodily movements to become ridiculous, so that your audience laughs at you. That is to cheapen and degrade the message. When movements detract the attention from the story to themselves, then you have gone too far. It is like everything else, we need to strike a balance: too much in either direction is wrong. But with the right amount of expression in the words, the voice and the body, the story can really live for the children.

With the Power of the Lord

Last of all, and most important, to tell a good story one should depend upon the Lord and not upon his own ability. The stories of the most educated are insipid without His help, and those of the willing ones without much training may be used to eternal glory if they are told in the power of His Holy Spirit. "Little is much if God is in it." Who knows what the simple telling of the gospel story shall mean to the boys and girls around about us?

> I love to tell the story,
> 'Twill be my theme in glory,
> To tell the old, old story
> Of Jesus and His love.

5

SONGS FOR CHILDREN

THE DAY of the triumphal entry little children were crying, "Hosanna to the son of David," and the chief priests and scribes asked Jesus to rebuke them. Instead, He commended them by saying, "Yea, have ye never read, Out of the mouth of babes and sucklings thou hast perfected praise?" Perfect praise comes from the lips of little children when they sing unto their Lord. We as teachers have a great responsibility in leading them in praising the Lord in song.

SELECTING THE SONGS

The message is of first importance in selecting the songs. Because the music furnishes an additional way to teach the children, we want to make sure that the words in each song are worthy of the time it takes to teach and to sing them. Will they impress more deeply some truth taught in the lesson, or will they indelibly print the words of a Bible verse on the child's heart? We have the children such a short time that each moment of time spent in class must be used to the greatest possible advantage. If some one unsaved hears the songs we have taught the children will he have a testimony of God's saving grace, or will he only hear foolish little nothings that we have unwisely selected to teach them? As well as having a message that would be a testimony to one who should overhear the child, the song should have in it that which means something to the child. One beautiful little crippled child who had attended a Child Evangelism Class went to the blackboard at school early one morning and drew a cross as she hummed, "On the Cross for me." Underneath it she wrote her name, "Donna." The teacher asked her what it meant, and she explained, "It means that Jesus died on the cross for Donna." The message of the song meant something to her.

The melody should also be considered in selecting the songs. Little children do not have a very wide range; that is, they are not capable of singing very low or very high, and a song which has a wide range is not suitable for the very little ones. Primary children have a slightly wider range, and the Junior child has a range still larger. Make sure that the song you want to teach is within the range of your children. The intervals (the jump from one note to the next) may be difficult in certain songs, and we must consider whether a song is worth the extra time it will take to teach the melody. Frequently excessive drill is required to see that the children sing the correct notes, and this is most unfortunate, as there are many songs which have such lilting melodies that they sing themselves right into the hearts of the children. And then, the rhythm must not be too complicated for the group. Of course as you teach the children song after song, they will be able to learn more difficult selections.

Little children like songs with motions, which the older ones are inclined to think babyish, but they all seem to enjoy songs which have a phrase repeated over and over. The "down in my heart" which is repeated in "I Have the Joy," makes it more attractive to children, as does the repetition of "rolling away" in "All of My Burdens Went Rolling Away." Notice a song which contains much repetition, and nine times out of ten it will be a child's favorite. The chorus of "Jesus Loves Me" in Chinese or some other foreign language makes a big hit with children of all ages. The following are a few of the many songs which children like.

Choruses

The B·I·B·L·E
Jesus Loves the Little Children
On the Cross for Me
'Tis Simple as Can Be
Into My Heart
Out of My Life *- INTO MY HEART*
Safe Am I
I'm So Happy
I Have the Joy
The Gospel Train
Gone, Gone, Gone
Rolled Away
All of My Burdens Went Rolling Away
Everything's All Right
Jesus Is the Sweetest Name I Know
V Is for Victory
No One Ever Cared for Me Like Jesus

Prayer Choruses

Into My Heart
Out of My Life
On the Cross for Me
Let the Beauty of Jesus Be Seen in Me

Scripture Choruses

I Am the Door
I Will Make You Fishers of Men
I'm Feeding on the Living Bread
Believe on the Lord Jesus Christ
Ye Must Be Born Again
For God So Loved the World
Thy Word Have I Hid in My Heart
I Am the Way
I Am the Resurrection and the Life

Hymns

Jesus Loves Me
I've Two Little Hands
We Are Little Soldiers
Onward Christian Soldiers
Fairest Lord Jesus
Whosoever Surely Meaneth
  Me
He Lives
Stand Up, Stand Up for
  Jesus

Trust and Obey
Standing on the Promises
The Bible Stands
Beautiful Words of Jesus
In My Heart There Rings a
  Melody
Holy, Holy, Holy

The teacher should have a few good chorus books such as "Salvation Songs for Children," "Singspiration Song Books," "The Pinebrook Chorus Books," and "Radio Songs and Choruses." If only one may be purchased, the first is to be preferred, as it is especially for children, while the others also contain songs for adults.

TEACHING THE SONGS

Start to teach the song by presenting the words along with a story, to illustrate a point. It may also be presented by some member of the class as a special number, or the pianist may use it as the music before or after class. Do not suddenly announce that the group is to learn a new song, but rather plan an approach from the children's activities, the change in seasons, the last lesson's review, or something near to the heart of the child which shall make him desire to learn the song. The pianist may play the melody as the children gather, or while they are bowing their heads for prayer. When she plays it for them to learn it she should play the melody in octaves that they may hear it better.

The rule of much repetition for learning applies to teaching songs as well as to memory work. We need to have as much variety here as there. The teacher may sing the song first, then have her helper or a child sing it with her. Next she may sing it, having the children hum. Then try it slowly with the children trying to sing. Post the words before the children on the blackboard, or have them printed with black crayon or India ink on blank newspaper or shirt cardboards. If the blank newspaper or cardboard is used, the copies should be saved for reviewing, or for helping new members learn the song. It is generally better to have the words before the whole class rather than for each member to have a book. This way the children become accustomed to looking up, and consequently singing out, and it is easier for the leader to direct them. Secure repetition by having the song sung by the first row, the last row, the ones who are six, seven, and eight, and the ones who are nine, ten, and eleven. Put in as many variations as you can devise.

No song should be taught without explaining the meaning. One little boy told his mother that they sang about the cross-eyed bear at Sunday school that morning. She and his teacher were both puzzled until they found that included in one song was the phrase, "The consecrated cross I'll bear." To make the meaning clear use pictures as much as possible. Holman Hunt's, "The Light of the World," is excellent to introduce "Into My Heart." Use a picture of a happy-faced child for "I'm So Happy," or "I Have the Joy." Jesus with the children of many lands is appropriate for "Jesus Loves the Little Children," while the Bible itself serves for "The B-I-B-L-E."

Some songs lend themselves to illustrating each phrase. In such a case a little booklet could be made and a child permitted to turn the page to show the picture as the song progressed. "Fairest Lord Jesus" can be treated in this manner.

> Fair are the *meadows,*
> Fairer still the *woodlands,*
> Robed in the *blooming garb of spring;*
> *Jesus* is fairer, Jesus is purer,
> Who makes the *woeful heart* to sing!

Most songs and choruses can be illustrated if a little imagination and diligence to find the pictures are employed.

LEADING THE SONGS

Many women are hesitant about standing in front of the children directing the music. They feel that since they have never done it that it is better for them not to try. The children do not know it is your first attempt, if you do not tell them. The first time is the hardest, so jump in and get it over with. However, there are some who just can't carry a tune. It is better for these to secure a helper, or to use the piano alone, or else have a musical child lead the singing. It really is amazing what a child can do when given the proper instruction. Perhaps some child in the group plays a musical instrument in a very acceptable fashion. He may lead with it. There are many ways for the teacher who is not talented to still have music in her class.

The piano should be placed so that the pianist can see the leader in order to better follow her. If the pianist must also lead, the piano should be placed so that she can see the children. She should not try to lead with her back.

It is of utmost importance for the leader to enjoy the singing. One song leader stood in front of a group of children with a face as expressive as a stove pipe, her mouth tightly locked, while she beat out the rhythm perfectly. The children were about as responsive as fence posts. Others have not known how to beat out the rhythm but have entered whole-heartedly into the singing, and the boys and girls nearly burst their throats for them. There are books on conducting which may be secured, and for the one who wishes to lead her own group it is helpful to remember that the first beat of every measure is indicated by a down stroke.

A theme—a thought around which the songs for a particular meeting or series of meetings are built—makes the music period more profitable, and prepares the way for the story or lesson. If you desire to have the children enter into the selection of the music, allow them to guess the hymn or chorus of which you are thinking after you have given them a broad hint. Make the motions to a chorus and let them guess it. This allows the carrying out of the theme, and yet permits child participation which is always valuable.

Let your class be divided in two, to introduce a little spice. One group starts the song, and in the middle the leader points to the other group, thus indicating that they shall carry it on. After a little practice you will be able to switch frequently from one side to the other to the keen delight of the children. This exercise may be used to emphasize the thought of the song. A special number by one member of the class, a duet, or a song by a small group all serve to make the singing more interesting.

Sing a few phrases in certain numbers softly and you will see that a more worshipful spirit results, and that more attention is paid to the message. The prayer chorus can be of great value in bringing about an attitude of worship. Use the same chorus for several months each time before prayer is offered. The children should bow their heads and close their eyes while they sing the chorus slowly and quietly.

There has been a trend in fundamental circles to use loud, peppy choruses almost entirely. A few of these do add zest, but we are robbing our children if our music is not balanced with the worshipful prayer chorus and the hymns of the church. In leading the music, let us see that a rounded-out selection of songs is made, bearing on the message of the day. Let us use some to give pep to the meeting, while through others we seek to maintain a spirit of quiet worship.

6

THE FLANNELGRAPH

DOES YOUR CLASS need renewed interest? Is it sometimes hard to keep the attention of your boys and girls? Are the children unable to remember what you told them last week? Then the answer to your problem is *the flannelgraph*. The results with boys and girls are startling. They are fascinated by the pictures "that won't fall over." Their minds and hearts are impressed by the truth more deeply when it enters the eye-gate as well as the ear-gate. And they remember — oh, how they remember! — the stories when told this new way. We are told that we remember 10% of what we hear, 50% of what we see, and 80% of what we see, hear, and do. The flannelgraph adapts itself to all of these. The child sees the story on the board before him, he hears the story from his teacher, and he "does" the story later when the teacher lets him review it on the flannel-graph. Thus it becomes a very part of him.

Most everyone now knows what the flannelgraph is—a method of portraying truth by means of pic-tures and objects pasted on flannel, which may be placed against an upright board covered with flannel. The flannel on the picture adheres to the flannel on the board, and the pictures remain in place. It is also referred to as the feltograph or flannel board.

Attendance in various classes has skyrocketed since the advent of this new method, teachers who before were mediocre have found new enthusiasm in their classes, and more boys and girls have been touched with the precious gospel of grace.

Because there are as many different ways of working with the flannelgraph as there are people who use it, different materials and methods will be discussed and the reader may decide which is most appropriate for him.

THE BOARD

Of the materials needed, the first to consider is a board. This may be as inexpensive as corrugated cardboard, or as elaborate as a board and easel together which fold as a suitcase. The cardboard, corrugated on both sides, may be taken from a large heavy grocery box and covered with black or gray flannel. Cut with a knife to 2x3 feet, and be sure the corners are square. The flannel may be glued on the back side of the board, but not on the front as that destroys its sticking qualities. Another piece of material a little less than 2x3 feet may be fastened to the back which will cover the raw edges and make a neater board. This board will be easy to carry, will not take much room to store, and with reasonable care will last a long time. Of course, a table is needed on which to place it while telling the story.

The folding easel and board is an advantage for the Christian worker who tells the story in many different places, where he will not always have a table. Material as well as the legs of the easel can be carried inside. The flannel is not already on these boards but must be put on after it is up. Use a couple of thumb tacks or a piece of flannel larger than the board so that a good bit of it will hang down in back. In this way no fasteners are needed. There are several different models on the market. Just remember that you will be carrying whatever it weighs and consider that. Many of them have a blackboard finish which is a very desirable feature. Time must be allowed before every meeting to assemble the board, but you will generally find in every group some mechanical boy who will delight to do the job for you. However, always supervise until the child learns how and you may save yourself some broken material.

Some one willing to spend a little time and a very little money may make a durable and satisfactory board from plywood, 2x3 feet. Paint it with blackboard enamel which may be purchased from a hardware or paint store. Thus, the blackboard may be used for the songs, puzzles, and memory verses, and with one yard square of flannel thrown over the board it is ready for the story. This size board is good, as yard wide flannel fits very nicely. If a larger board is used the material must be cut the lengthwise of the goods and much more is required. However, this size is good for the small and medium sized figures, and can be used with the larger figures. Some use a board 3x4 feet for the larger figures. An audience up to 250 or 300, if seated close together, can see the figures on the small board. For ordinary class work and children's meetings these are recommended. The traveling children's evangelist who gets the very best equipment will prefer the large figures and board. If extremely large groups of children are contacted, he may prefer even a larger board.

THE SCENES

What kind of background shall I use? This is one of the first questions. For you who are beginning with a new set of children and have all the work of preparing figures for the first time, plain black flannel or vello cloth will be very satisfactory. The bright colored figures show up well against it, and the children will like it even if the scene is not worked out. As time goes on you can get a few scenes, but this is not necessary to start. One of the first scenes should be a general outdoor one which can be used for most Bible stories. This may be just a general landscape with mountains or hills in the background. One method consists in cutting various strips of flannel or vello cloth and building the scene before the children. Thus one strip would be green for the grass, another blue for the sky, and a third dark blue or purple for the hills. Other pieces may be used for a lake, mountains may be omitted, and a stretch of oriental houses substituted. This way several pieces of flannel or vello are used for one scene. They may be interchanged with other sets of scenery. For instance, the tan ground of a desert scene may be used with the blue sky of the regular scene. An orange sunset sky may be used with a seaside scene. The advantage of this method is its interchangeability, but the disadvantage is that it is quite difficult to keep track of each separate piece, and sometimes takes considerable time to decide just which pieces to use.

The Mead scenes are of this type and are very attractive in vello cloth. Vello cloth is a new cloth quite superior to flannel, in that it does not wrinkle easily and has more body than flannel. One side is not fuzzy, but objects adhere nevertheless. This side is used for the drawing and the results are much nicer than when flannel is used.

The Munn scenes are beautiful indeed, but out of the reach of the pocketbook of most children's workers. They are drawn on wool felt, and felt fig-ures come with every scene. They are so constructed that they may be used on both sides, which really cuts the price in two, making them cost about the same as the Mead scenes. For a special occasion one of these scenes would add a beauty and dignity that would not soon be forgotten by the audience. And anyone who can afford them for all flannelgraph work certainly has great cause to rejoice.

Using a yard of unbleached muslin, white flannel, or vello cloth, and drawing a complete scene on it with crayon, payons or oils, is another way to make a background. This may be done by the teacher or some artistic child or friend. The beautiful pictures on Beginner and Primary leaflets furnish many sug-gestions for making backgrounds. These may be copied by one who has no artistic talent, or who has never done any drawing. It does take quite a bit of time, but because the flannel especially permits new lines on top of mistakes, without showing, it is pos-sible for an amateur to get satisfactory results by copying from a good picture. Most people are afraid to try. If you don't have the money to buy a scene, do try to make one. Or get some one else to try for you. Is there a scene outside the temple? Find a picture with a temple in it, and seek to copy it. Notice each detail. Do not be dismayed because the task seems too big. Ask the Lord to help you. The author has absolutely no artistic talent, but has amazed herself at what a little time and application will do. One thing, remember both scenes and figures should not be too brilliant in color, as they may clash when put together. Consider what the total effect will be rather than concentrating on making one item.

These scenes drawn all in one piece are somewhat easier to use and are more convenient for the teacher. They do not provide quite as much interest for the children as the other type, but are very satisfactory. Of course, they may be used over and over again.

For an easy-to-make night scene, take a yard of dark blue and paste a few packaged stars in the sky. Cut a circle or crescent from gold paper for the moon, and the children are transported into long-ago night with Jacob or Nicodemus.

For one who has not begun the flannelgraph work, this may sound confusing. Just remember that the only scene you need to start with is a piece of black. The children's imagination will supply trees, sky, mountains, etc.

THE FIGURES

Although a great variety of figures for Bible stories are now available, it is generally best for the beginner to choose those figures which come with the stories already written. In this way he secures additional help and instructions, and is started on this new way of Bible teaching with much more ease. After he has become accustomed to teaching the flannelgraph way he will wish to get additional figures even though the stories do not accompany them. Out of his own experience and Bible study he will be able to co-ordinate the figures with the story.

The majority of figures are 9-11 inches in height, which is ideal for the board 2 by 3 feet. The larger figures are good for some special occasion or for the meetings where over one hundred children attend. They may also be used with a small group but are not necessary. The cost is considerably more. The small figures may also be used with an audience up to about three or four hundred, but the larger ones would be preferred for that size group. The following chart may help in selecting your material.

Material	Producer	Size	Price
Figures with stories for books as "Gospel of John," "Genesis," etc.	Irene B. Ranny	9-11 in.	moderately priced
Figures, not stories, following themes, such as "Life of Christ."	Hollenbeck	9-11 in.	moderately priced
Figures for individual stories — no stories furnished.	Story-O-Graph	15-20 in.	more expensive

One nice thing about the flannelgraph is that the materials may be used over and over again in new ways. Rebecca with her pot may also be the woman at the well; Miriam watching the baby Moses may in another setting become the little maid who told Naaman's wife of her God. Abraham may pose as Moses, and innumerable Bible characters may on the flannelgraph play a double role. Of course, care must be taken not to have the figure take on a new personality too soon or the children will discover the ruse.

As to the preparation: color the figures first, glue flannel to the back, dry thoroughly, and last of all cut out. If the figures are cut out before they are dry, the likelihood is that the figure will curl. The completed sheet may be placed under the rug, or the sheet cut into sections and placed in a very large book to dry.

The figures may be colored with crayons, water colors, or show card colors. The crayons are the least desirable, and the show card colors the most desirable. I have seen work done beautifully in crayons, and some done in show card colors that left very much to be desired. Every one improves with practice no matter what medium is used. Show card colors are also called tempera paints, and poster paints. They come in bottles, may be thinned in water for tints, or mixed with other colors for different shades. When, after standing a long time, they become thick, add water and let stand overnight. With red, yellow, blue, black, and white, almost every different color is possible. However, if much of this work is done the painter will wish to buy the additional bottles to save the time of mixing the colors.

Mixing Chart	*Minimum colors needed*
Red and yellow—orange	Red
Red and blue—purple	Yellow
Yellow and blue—green	Blue
Red and white—pink	White
Blue and white—pale blue	Black
Purple and white—lavender	
Black and white—gray	
Red and yellow and small amount blue—brown	
Brown and white—tan	
Red and yellow and white—flesh color	

Beautiful pastels may be made by adding white to any given color. Jar lids make excellent containers in which to mix the paint. Not much is required for painting quite a bit, but be sure to mix enough as it is difficult to match a color that has been mixed. Flesh color may be made by mixing red, yellow, and white. Pink is not a real flesh color. Take a look at your own arm when trying to mix flesh color. Remember also that the outdoor fishermen and sheep-herder were somewhat darker than we are. Crayons may be used one color on top of another and rubbed with the finger tip to secure a smooth blend.

One tip which has been helpful to many who are not artistically inclined is to make the folds of the garment darker than the garment itself if the figures are not shaded. If they are shaded, the shaded part should be colored darker than the remainder of the garment. Most people figure as I did. If a dress is red, it is red all over. But to the eye it does not appear this way. The folds seem to be a darker red. Where there are lines in the garment, paint this line a darker color, and you will be pleased with the result. This shading may occur in the skirts, the head-dress, the hair, the sashes, and even in the hands, if they are prominent in the scene. Wherever there would be shadows, these places should be painted a darker shade of the same color. Do not worry about this too much at first, but do the best you can. The Lord made things beautiful when He made this earth, and I believe that He would be honored with figures neatly done and true to life. Many suggestions may be gained by studying the work of the masters.

Coat the back of the sheet of figures with a liquid glue and press flannel against it. Some say that the figures should be mounted on a heavier paper or cardboard before gluing to flannel, but very satisfactory results are obtained if flannel completely covers the back of the figure. The extra weight of the cardboard sometimes causes the figure to fall from the board. Then, too, a figure with just flannel on the back may be bent to carry from place to place, or to store, and will not leave a crease as would the cardboard. The flannel must completely cover the back of the figure. Of course, scraps may be used for the work of backing the figures, and it does not matter what color or what quality flannel. Some one who has been sewing for a baby may have an abundance of flannel to donate. Remember to completely dry the figures after painting and gluing before cutting them out. It helps to either number the figure or to write the name of the character on the back.

There is no use denying it, a great deal of work is required to prepare the scenes and figures for the flannelgraph, but anyone who has used it over a period of time will testify that it is well worth the trouble. In some cities the women who are teaching classes get together for an all-day meeting and prepare figures together. If the gathering has been well planned and all materials are present and ready to be used, a great deal can be accomplished in a pleasant way. In other cities the women set aside part of August and prepare their figures for most of the year to come. Where these groups work together so well, why could not a library of figures be established? All the figures required for one story could be placed in one envelope, with a smaller envelope and card placed on the outside as is contained in a library book. One of the women could be librarian, and send out notices for stories overdue, or see that none were lost. To get such a collection, no one would be permitted to borrow any stories until he had contributed a certain number of stories. These could be inspected by a committee each year, or more frequently, as decided by the group. Each member could be taxed another story, and thus the collection would grow and be more useful. After joining the group the stories would no longer belong to the maker but to the group. In this way a great deal of use could be derived from the figures made. One person could be assigned to inspect the figures frequently, so that soiled ones would be discarded.

To store the figures, manila folders, or large envelopes may be used. These may be labeled on the flap or front as to what story is contained. You will soon find that there are some figures which are used frequently. It is a question whether to store such a figure with one story and remember which one it is with, or to store all such versatile figures in one folder by themselves. The latter seems to be the more satisfactory.

Let no one think that just because he uses the flannelgraph souls will be saved, and that if he does not use it souls will not be saved. God works through a clean vessel to give forth His Word in the power of the Holy Spirit. If our hearts are not clean, if we do not give forth the pure Word of God, and if we do not go forth in the power of the Holy Spirit, we can make figures until we are blue in the face for all it will prosper the work of God. This is a means that has been used of the Lord, it is worth the time and the trouble, and you will find that it does fascinate children. We must, however, look to the Lord to work in the hearts and lives of the children, depend upon Him for the message and expect Him to bring about the results.

7

MEETINGS FOR CHILDREN

HAVE YOU been asking yourself the question, "How can I best win children for the Lord Jesus?" If you have, you will be interested in the different avenues of approach that the Lord has been pleased to honor in this work for Him. They range from the most simple, with no organization at all, to a complex campaign with many factors taken into account.

PERSONAL WORK

First of all is the most simple, that of speaking to children wherever we come in contact with them: on the bus, out in the park, on our front lawn, or out in a vacant lot. In other words, it is personal work with boys and girls. The Lord has blessed this method in a remarkable way when accompanied by consistent prayer. One worker spent ten weeks on the streets of Chicago speaking to little groups of children on the streets, and over five thousand professed to receive Christ as Saviour. The ordinary lay person cannot spend a full day speaking to children as he finds them, but he will meet with children occasionally, and he may ask God to enable him to speak with them about the Lord Jesus Christ, and seek to lead them to a knowledge of Him. Thus, the

ordinary contacts of life are turned to eternal advantage.

A notable work along this line has been done with
the children in Chicago for the past several years.
As soon as the weather is warm enough for children
to be out, the city is honeycombed with a band of
workers speaking to the children. The city is divided
into sections of several blocks each and portions of
parks and beaches to which volunteer workers are
assigned. Each one goes to his section once a week
for an hour or so with the wordless book, the gospel
walnut, or just the simple message of salvation. No
meetings are held; no songs are sung. Quietly, effectively, children are made friends with, told the gospel
story, and invited to come to the Saviour. Many and
wonderful are the tales told by these workers. One
young woman reported that she stayed for two and
one-half hours on one street corner telling the gospel
over and over again. She stepped from the street car,
reached the curb, and there was a girl about ten
years of age. She made friends with her and led her
to the Saviour. This child, glowing with joy, said
eagerly, "Don't go away, I want you to tell my pals
about this." She disappeared for a moment, and re-
turned bringing three or four children her own age.
As soon as she saw that they were accepting the
message, she disappeared again only to reappear with
a new batch of recruits. This went on and on until
the worker had stayed much longer than she had
planned, and still the child was bringing more. That
day on one street corner many, many children
entered into a new life with Christ.

Another worker went to the colored section once
each week. She met a little colored boy named

George, who seemed intensely interested. After he had accepted Christ, he asked question after question. Mrs. Harvey (not her real name) sat down with him under a tree and showed him the answers to his questions in her Bible. She told us afterward that she thought she told him all she knew. He was captivated by the wordless book and asked her where he could get one. Very generously she gave him hers. The next week she came back to the same section and saw three children playing. After talking with them awhile she asked, "Have you ever seen a book without words?" This was the way she opened the conversation about the Lord. What was her surprise to hear them say, "Yes, we have." She knew that she was the only worker assigned to that section and she could not imagine how they had seen one.

"George showed one to us," they told her.

Mrs. Harvey, however, told the story again, thanking the Lord for giving her cultivated ground, but she was not prepared for what she found.

"Wouldn't you like to ask Jesus to come into your hearts so that He could make them nice and clean?" she asked.

"Oh, we already did that," they explained.

"When did you?"

"Why, when George showed us his wordless book he told us to ask Jesus to come into our hearts, and He would make us happy. And we did, and He did."

Little George had already become a soul winner. Oh, that adult converts were as zealous.

Of course, personal work with children is not a bed of roses. There are many difficulties. Sometimes when leaders of strong church groups not holding to the truth have found that their children have had a new experience, they warn the other children in the vicinity, forbidding them to listen to a stranger. Many hardships have thus been encountered, but when backed by persistent, prevailing prayer, even these have been overcome. However, this is a difficulty that does not arise until this type of work has been done over a period of years in a single city. If you are just starting this work, you will not have this to fight.

There will be one thing which will greatly hinder those who have the desire to do this type of work. That is the failure to begin. The prospective worker knows not what is ahead of him and often Satan prevents him from ever beginning by filling his heart with fear, or by bringing one thing or another to his attention which should be done instead of contacting the children. Because of this, the best way for beginners is to set a definite time when two will go together. If one person has done the work before, he can take a new one with him; otherwise they may both begin together.

The disadvantage of this plan of winning the children is that Satan seeks to prevent the worker from doing it at all, and the advantage is that it is one of the most fruitful ministries to children. We have observed that sometimes teachers, who are able to lead large groups of children, organize Daily Vacation Bible Schools, and conduct successful meetings for boys and girls, are very often afraid to get started in this work. They confess that they do not know what to say. On the other hand, some of the very best workers in this field have been exceedingly timid folk, those who never speak out in meetings, and are so quiet that no one even knows they are around.

Do not despair if you are timid. Perhaps this is the ministry God has for you.

In England a work very similar to this has been done for many years by the Children's Special Service Mission. Recently a missionary from China told us that the majority of the missionaries in her mission were saved on the streets of England under this plan. She had visited in many of their homes and said that their parents were of the extremely worldly type. They themselves were saved while children because they were contacted on the street by an interested Christian, and when they grew up their lives were spent for God on the foreign field. Truly a marvelous testimony of how God keeps His children. For more information about this field of service see the book, "Open Air Child Evangelism," by J. Irvin Overholtzer, Child Evangelism Fellowship.

THE SUNDAY SCHOOL

Eternity alone will reveal what has been accomplished for God in the Sunday school. It was as a result of the Sunday school and a consecrated teacher doing God's task that D. L. Moody was brought to Christ. If this were the only result we would not be able even then to estimate the worth of the Sunday school to the kingdom of God. The Sunday school has contacted those who would not otherwise have been reached by the church, and the church has profited by their presence and help later on. Many children of unsaved parents are contacted in this way, and through them the parents are reached.

In this modern world of growth and development communities have been known to spring up almost overnight. A new subdivision is opened, a housing project is built, a group of homes grow up around a new industry, the opening of a new defense plant brings people to a new locality.

Soon grocery stores, drug stores, filling stations, and other commercial establishments are available to the newcomers. They also need a testimony to the saving grace of the Lord Jesus, but all too often it is several years before this is effected. Do you live in or near one of these places? Perhaps the Lord would have you organize a Sunday school. Even if you have never done it before, God will honor your efforts if they are backed with much prayer. If there are other Christians willing to help, they might gather together for prayer several times before plans are discussed. "Except the Lord build the house they labor in vain that build it." Because a Sunday school is more or less of a community project there will be many in favor of it who do not know the Word of God, or perhaps are not saved. It is of utmost importance that they are not placed in a position of authority, and for this reason a groundwork of prevailing prayer needs to be laid before anything else is done.

Next, a place of meeting may be selected. It may be an empty store building, a home with large rooms, or perhaps the school. This, too, should be a matter of prayer. Then a few teachers should be selected. It is better to have one good teacher than many poor ones. Never let a person teach who is not saved. The blind cannot lead the blind. If possible, it is best to have the children separated from the adults. However, it may be at first that most of the Sunday school will be children, and they may be divided accordingly. The time of meeting may be Sunday morning, or in many cases, Sunday afternoon. Take into consideration the habits of the community, and try to set a time when the most people can come.

After the time and place have been set, call on the different homes in the community with a cordial invitation to attend the first meeting. A special attraction will aid in getting more to come out, but nothing takes the place of personal interest. After the call, send a card urging the attendance of the family. A poster or two in the stores will help, as will a news item in the newspaper that serves the community.

But if there are no facilities such as these available, do not despair. On the lawn of one housing project in Chicago a Sunday school was carried on all summer with an average attendance of from eighty-five to one hundred.

One thing to watch in starting a community Sunday school is that all officers, teachers, and those who have to do with the work are saved, and that they are true to the Word of God. A person, no matter how well educated and well qualified in other respects, has no place in a position of authority in an organization whose purpose is to lead men to a Saviour he does not know. Pray earnestly that the Sunday school may be kept for God, and may not degenerate into a community social affair.

The program for the new Sunday school need not be complex, in fact, it is better to start out simply, being sure to keep it Christ-centered and true to the Bible. The meeting may well start with group singing. You will be fortunate if you are able to secure a piano, but do not use a pianist unless he is able to play the correct notes and keep the proper rhythm.

Nothing is more embarrassing than to try to lead a group in singing while the pianist stumbles along hunting for the next note. The best thing to do in such a case is to sing without accompaniment. You may be able to borrow enough hymn books from some interested church, but in case you are not, the words may be printed on a blackboard, or if even that is not available, they may be put on blank news-paper with heavy black crayon, show card color, or India ink. Save all copies for future use. Someone who is handy with tools might make an easel where they could be kept and displayed.

The program may be outlined as follows:

> 20 minutes Gospel singing
> 10 minutes Special feature
> 5 minutes Scripture reading and prayer
> 40 minutes Classes with study of the Scripture lesson
>
> ---
>
> 1 hour, 15 minutes—Total Time

This is only a suggestion, and of course, may be altered to suit the individual case. The special feature adds much interest to the Sunday school. It may consist of an object lesson, a flannelgraph talk, a special musical number, or a blackboard talk.

Here then, is thrown out briefly an idea which, if developed, will bring true blessing and salvation to many who otherwise might not hear. Is God speaking to you about your community? Ask Him what He would have you do about those who live near you.

Additional information may be secured by writing to the American Sunday School Union, 1816 Chest-nut Street, Philadelphia, Pa.

THE CHILD EVANGELISM CLASS OR BIBLE CLUB

During the past several years a new method for winning children to Christ has sprung up—The Bible Club. Boys and girls are gathered into homes right after school one day a week for an hour in which they sing gospel songs, learn memory verses, listen to a Bible story which contains the gospel, and receive an invitation to accept Christ as Saviour.

Advantages

Catholic children forbidden to enter a Protestant church, Jewish children, boys and girls with atheistic parents, and those whose parents simply neglect their spiritual instruction, meet in a neighborhood home with children who *do* go to Sunday school but receive very little biblical instruction, and others who attend good sound Sunday schools. What an opportunity! Some of these children could never be brought into a church to hear the gospel, but a woman in their own neighborhood, across whose lawn they have run many times, invites them into her home, and they meet there around God's precious Word. They meet with children on the same social level. If the neighborhood is a poor one and the home is very simple, the children do not mind—that is the type of home they have, too. On the other hand, if the home is pretentious, the children are comfortable, for they live in the same district and come from similar homes.

Many children are not in Sunday school today because indifferent parents will not make the effort to arise early enough on Sunday to get them ready.

Many of these parents are not actually antagonistic to spiritual things, but just neglect them. Their children can be reached through the Bible Club, as it requires no effort on the parents' part for the child to attend a club right after school. He does not have to change his clothes, he does not have to bring an offering, and furthermore, he is out from under foot for another hour.

Since the home does not carry a distinct denominational mark, many children come who could not go to a church carrying a "Baptist," "Methodist," or "Presbyterian" name. These are a few of the advantages of the Bible Club.

Asks H. G. Wells, "Is there, after forty, any alternative to bridge?" And he answers thus: "At present there is no useful role for most of these women in their forties and fifties. Their old jobs, if they had jobs before marriage, do not want them back."

Life Begins at Forty—by Walter B. Pitkin.

No useful role, when boys and girls are without Christ on their very doorsteps? No useful role, when hungry-hearted children are longing for the Bread of life, and there is none to give unto them? Their old jobs may not want these women back, but God wants them. He wants to use them as laborers in His harvest. Are you over forty and feel unwanted? Listen to His call: "It is not the will of your Father which is in heaven, that one of these little ones should perish" (Matt. 18:14). Are there lost little ones near you? Then He would have you go to them and tell them of His love, and gather them into His fold. Christ has a work for you to do. Women over forty have played a very definite part in the Bible Club movement that is sweeping the country. They have become hostesses, teachers, have organized the work in new sections, and have even become State Directors. Yes, the Bible Club has another advantage; it offers to women over forty a new life of service.

One church found, after experimenting with starting new Sunday schools in outlying communities, that they could reach more children by having week-day Home Bible Clubs instead. The classes were started, held several weeks, calls made on the parents, and finally an invitation extended for the family to attend the main Sunday school. After the parents were acquainted with the teacher and realized that their children were benefiting from the classes, denominational barriers that might have interfered were broken down, and permission was granted for the children to attend. The Sunday school which used this plan would receive eight, ten, twelve, and even twenty new members on a single Sunday. As the Sunday school is a feeder for the church, so the Child Evangelism Class is a feeder for the Sunday school. Through the efforts of one unassuming Christian woman on the north side of Chicago, forty children were added to the Sunday school. Another woman during the three years in which she had a Bible Club, brought sixty-five children into the Sunday school of her choice. A missionary to Guatamala, where the Bible Clubs have been started, stated that their mission reached more children through Bible Clubs in homes than they did in the Sunday school.

Some women have neglected to invite the children in their Bible Club to Sunday school and church. This is very definitely a mistake. The saved child needs to be affiliated with the church. It is one more tie which links him to God. He has enough pulls in the other direction to need every tie possible to bind him closer to the Lord. One teacher asks at the opening of each Bible Club period how many children attended Sunday school that week, and those attending receive a bright gold star. If the teacher's or hostess' Sunday school is too far distant from the child's home, she could give his name to a teacher in a nearby Sunday school, and encourage her to contact the child for that Sunday school.

One hostess invited the children who lived in the next apartment to her Child Evangelism Class. The children were saved, and then she invited them to Sunday school. Each Sunday her family was accompanied by the two neighborhood youngsters, as they went on the street car to Sunday school. One day their mother passed her in the hall. "Mrs. Brown, my husband and I don't go to Sunday school anywhere. Next Sunday you go with us in our car to Sunday school, and all the children can ride too." Thus two adults were brought under the sound of the testimony.

Time and Place

As has already been stated, classes generally meet in homes one day a week right after school. However, this is not a hard and fast rule. Some mothers have found it more convenient to hold the class on Saturday mornings, while in other localities Sunday afternoons seemed the best time. In some sections there are no homes available, and the clubs meet in a co-operating church or mission. The plan is elastic enough to allow it to be adapted to the community.

Materials

Only the simplest materials are necessary to conduct a Bible Club. A place with chairs and a piano is an ideal set-up. One class which had more children than chairs was helped when the hostess borrowed several table boards and made benches by placing the boards between chairs. True, there was scarcely enough room for the teacher to stand in the room when all the children had assembled, but what did it matter when little souls were saved each week? Another hostess substituted orange crates for chairs, while in another home the children used the floor. One father with kindly thoughts for the children built little benches which were used for this purpose. The basement was all fitted out just for the Bible Club. A flannelgraph board was built on the wall, pictures were hung, an old piano was secured, and the children had a room for their own. Some women have the children meet in their bright kitchens where tracks may be easily mopped. Another woman stands at the front door with a broom, and brushes off the children who have been romping in the snow. Covers are put over the upholstered furniture before the children arrive, and are taken off after they leave. And as to the piano, that is not really necessary. In fact, the majority of classes in some sections do not have one. Most of these classes sing a capello, but others are led by a child who plays a musical instrument. He may be informed beforehand what songs are to be sung and thus can practice. Do not use a child, however, unless he can play the correct notes and keep the right rhythm, as he will hinder rather than help. Some have a piano but no pianist. Others have earnestly desired a piano for their class and have taken the matter to the Lord in prayer. Over and over again He has answered this prayer to glorify His name. Many people no longer want their upright pianos and will give them away if they are moved. If you feel you must have a piano pray earnestly about the matter and God will surely hear. One class has met for four years and has never had a piano or any musical instrument. The class averages from twenty-five to forty. Thus, you see it is not an absolute necessity.

Besides these things, the teacher will need lesson helps for teaching. These should be purchased from the Child Evangelism Fellowship, 203 N. Wabash Ave., Chicago, Illinois. Ordinary lessons are not used, but special stories have been prepared in which the gospel is given each time. This is the most important required material. A class should not be started until this material is secured, as just the telling of a Bible story, or the teaching of what the teacher knows about the Bible will not generally result in the salvation of souls, and that is the purpose of the class. Do not fail to secure this material. In the author's opinion, it is the best material available for children's work. A Bible Club is not a true Bible Club unless literature from the Child Evangelism Fellowship is used. A song or chorus book may be obtained from the above address or at any good publishing house selling Christian literature. Inexpensive awards may be used to build up the class or to aid in memory work, but are not an absolute necessity. A flannelgraph board which has a blackboard finish is a great help in the work, but should not be considered essential. Flannelgraph material was discussed in a previous chapter.

How to Conduct a Bible Club

Prayer

Every Bible Club should be started in prayer. So many factors enter in, and Satan hates this work to such an extent that every part of it must be fortified in prayer. It is important that the right hostess and teacher are mated; therefore this should be made a matter of prayer. Difficulties can arise from placing the wrong people together, either one of whom would work perfectly well with someone else. Pray too that the right children will come to the Club, those whose hearts are prepared for the message of salvation. One little skeptic might throw cold water over the interest of a whole group, especially at the first. As the first meeting of the Club more or less sets the stage for future meetings, it is of utmost importance that this meeting go off well. Pray about the discipline: that the children will behave, and that they will be interested to such an extent that no behaviour problems will arise. Let us remember, too, that God answers the requests that we *make,* so let us include all the requests. The ladies interested in one class prayed about the things mentioned above, and God answered those prayers in a wonderful manner. But after the class a friend asked, "Were any children saved at that meeting?" The answer was "No." Then the ladies suddenly realized that they had not asked God to save souls at that meeting, although that was the whole reason they had begun the Child Evangelism Class. They quickly brought that request to Him, and the next time could report several boys and girls brought to the Saviour. Nothing is too small to bring to Him. If some particular phase of the meeting will be hard for you, pray earnestly about it, and ask your friends to do the same. Then give Him the glory when He brings the victory. The wonderful thing about having a Bible Club is seeing so very many answers to prayer. Prayer is the foundation, not only of the beginning of the Bible Club, but also remains the basis for it as long as it continues.

Preparation

Next, the day and time should be chosen. If the Boy or Girl Scouts meet on Wednesday, or baseball practice is on Wednesday, it would be the part of wisdom not to choose that day. If you are able, find out about the school activities and choose a day when the most children can attend. Also be careful not to choose a holiday to start your class, as the children's schedule is upset and they will not remember to come. The time should be set right after school, so that the children will not have time to return home. Otherwise they may find something else to engage their interest. Also, it might be well to say that a home near the school is a very wise choice, since it is available to the greatest number of children.

Now, the children must be invited to the Club. If you know the children in the neighborhood, contact them personally. You may also call on their mothers, explaining that this is an interdenominational effort, that the doctrines of any particular church are not taught, but that the children are told stories from the Bible and that an effort is made from these stories to have an effect on their conduct. However, the way most classes secure their first group of children is to have some one pass out colored invitations (which contain the place and time of meeting) at the school as the children leave. There are different ways to pass out these invitations and they bring as many different results. One person may resemble a telephone pole as far as coldness, aloofness, and interest in the children is concerned. Others let their love for the children be felt. They are warm and friendly, seeing each child as an individual. It isn't difficult to see which one has the most at her Bible Club. Some states prohibit the passing out of literature on the school grounds. Therefore station yourself on the sidewalk in front of the school or even across the street. If the home where the class is to be held is north of the school, pick the north corner to pass out the invitations. One teacher wondered why no one responded to all the invitations she passed out, and finally discovered that she had chosen the wrong corner. All the children who passed that way lived in the opposite direction, and the Club was too far for them.

Then do not think that because you pass out fourteen invitations, fourteen little darlings will show up. You will need many times that number of invitations to get fourteen children. Invitation blanks may be secured from the Child Evangelism Fellowship. Do not leave the filling out of the blanks until the last minute, because it really takes longer than one would expect. Some like to design their own and have them printed as blotters. In my opinion, it is better to pass out invitations at least two different times, as this will fix the matter in the child's mind. One of these should be as the children go home for lunch on the day your class is to start. The boys and girls may then ask permission of their parents, and yet do not have such a long time in which to forget about the Club. The more you work with children, the more you will find out what short memories they have. Do not give them a chance to forget. It often helps, at least for the first few times, for the teacher or some one interested in the class to be on a certain corner across from the school to walk with the children. When they see her they are reminded that it is Bible Club day, and they will come.

Besides preparing to have the children there, the teacher will need to have her program prepared. She must know what she is going to do each minute of the time that the children are there in order to use the time to the best advantage, and in order that the children do not become unruly. Given below is a sample of what might be done the first time the Bible Club meets.

> Welcome the children
> Teach the chorus "The B-I-B-L-E"
> Teach John 3:16
> Tell the story of the wordless book
> Give the invitation for the children to come to Christ
> Close with a brief prayer

Later on the Bible Club hour should be divided as follows:

> 15 minutes   Gospel singing
> 15 minutes   Memory work
> 20 minutes   Bible story
> 10 minutes   Invitation and closing prayer

If you do not already know the chorus, of course you should learn it and learn it well. If you have a blackboard, print the words in large letters before the class meets. Paint a piece of plywood two by three feet with blackboard paint bought at a paint or hardware store. However, if you do not wish to do this, a shirt cardboard with a black crayon will do just as well. This can be saved and used later to review the song, or when new children come.

Slips of colored construction paper may be prepared with the memory verse for the following week written or typed on them. If they are colored the children are not so apt to lose them.

Then the teacher must prepare the story. It is well to start each class with the wordless book if the children are not familiar with it, as this illustrates the gospel so well. The teacher should look up verses on heaven, sin, the Cross, salvation, until they become a very part of her. No matter what the story is, she should first study the Bible. She should meditate upon the verses. If she wishes to use an illustration, she should get all the details clearly in her mind. As she does the dishes or walks to the store, she should see if she can recall the story in its proper sequence, until she can do so without difficulty. She may tell the story to her son or to a niece for practice, or tell it aloud by herself for the first few times. She may also plan just how she will phrase the words of the invitation. Later these things will come naturally, but the first time this practice is very helpful.

As part of her preparation, the teacher should arrive early at the place where she is to teach, so that she can help arrange the chairs for the children and decide where she will stand. In a home, there may be several places where she may stand, and she should decide beforehand which would be best, rather than waiting, and then causing the children to move.

If there are two or three adults, the duties may be divided. One person may take the names and addresses at a table by the door as the children come in. This is the ideal way, as the getting of this information is anything but interesting and makes the class time dull to the children, besides creating unnecessary discipline problems. Later, the children can say their memory verses at the door as well as being checked for attendance there. If there is no adult available for this, an older girl who can be trusted may be trained to do it. If you have some one interested in the Bible Club work but who declares that she cannot do anything to help, ask her to take the attendance and hear the memory verses, and she will soon learn by observation how the class is conducted, and later may be willing to teach a class. Many good teachers have been trained into the work in this way. After she has been helping for a while ask her if she would like to bring an object lesson or conduct a drill for the children. The person who takes the attendance should not be the one who leads the singing, as it is often necessary to start before all the children have arrived, and she cannot be doing two things at once. If you have enough help, let one person play the piano while another leads the singing. Many Bible Clubs have only one adult—she takes attendance, plays the piano, leads the singing, hears the memory work, and tells the story. It is possible, but it is much easier if she can secure a helper or two. The teacher should decide upon and arrange for each one of these tasks beforehand, in order that the class will move smoothly.

Presentation

It is now time for the children to come. Every-thing insofar as is possible is ready. Time has been spent in prayer, the hostess and teacher are leaning hard on the Lord for strength. As the children arrive, make them feel at home. Remember this is a new experience for them, too. You want it to be pleasant so that they will return. If you are cordially inter-ested in them they will sense it, and will like to come to the Child Evangelism Class. You will probably be surprised to learn how little love some children get at home. Welcome the children not only with words, but also with your attitude.

In teaching the chorus, let the pianist play it as the children assemble, and they will become familiar with the melody before they have learned the words. A few words about the song, making it interesting and explaining the meaning, will make the children want to learn it. Sing it for them a couple of times even if you do not have a remarkable voice. They won't mind, and you will soon learn not to. Then let them hum it while you sing it again. Have them try it slowly as you point to the words. If there are enough children, have the girls sing it, then the boys, then have them stand and sing it. Vary the conditions under which they sing the song, and have them do it several times, and they will enjoy learning it.

The same idea can also be used in teaching the memory verse. The blackboard method is good to use the first time. See the chapter on memory work. As for the story, it should be made as inter-esting as possible. The best way to do this is to be interested yourself. Do not read the story. Do not keep a quarterly or book in your hand. If you must have help, write your outline on a small slip of paper and put it in your Bible, but only refer to it in an emergency. There is no easier way to kill interest in the Bible Club than to read the story. Never do that. It is almost the unpardonable sin. Let each person speak in the words he might have used. Use direct quotations rather than indirect. It is more powerful. One child always looked over a library book to see if it had lots of quotation marks before selecting it. The story with the most quotation marks is more interesting to them. Stick close to the facts given in Scripture. Too much imagination is not good. Unless you have had experiece in story telling, it is better to tell a short story first and hold the attention, than to drag it out and lose it. Later on increase the length of the story.

As you near the end of the story proceed naturally into the invitation. Give the children a fair opportunity to accept the Lord as their Saviour, but do not beg them, or look disapprovingly upon them if they do not wish to receive Christ. After the first meeting it is better to deal with the children right in the presence of the others, as a large percentage of the group generally will respond unless it is a group which has already been evangelized.

Dismiss the children with a few cordial words, telling them that you will be looking for them the next week at the same time.

If all these instructions have been followed as unto the Lord and in His strength, we are sure that you will have cause to praise Him after your first class is over. Your soul will be refreshed, and His joy will be bubbling over in your heart. Why wait any longer to start YOUR class?

Questions and Answers

Question: What shall I do when my class becomes too large? If I speak so that the little ones understand, the older ones become bored.

Answer: Have the singing and memory work with the whole group taking part, but sepaarte the group for the story, putting the little ones in the dining room or bedroom with another teacher. The class may even be divided into three groups, according to ages. One moderately sized home had a class of sixty-five which met in the combined dining and living room. When story time came the little ones went into the kitchen, the older ones in the bedroom, and the middle sized group stayed in the living room. The memory work might also be taken care of in these smaller groups.

If the teacher preferred, the group might be separated by having the girls meet on one day and the boys on another. In this way the same teacher could teach all the children, which would be an advantage in case of shortage of teachers.

Question: Should I serve refreshments?

Answer: Generally the answer is "No." It is not necessary. The children will come without it if properly trained. They will enjoy awards for memory work even more. There is an abiding value if awards which contain the Scripture are chosen. Refreshments take valuable time from the Bible Club proper, which is much more important. The children may soil their clothes, and thus the ill-will of some mothers will be secured. It is far better to omit the refreshments altogether, and have a real party for the children once or twice a year with games and refreshments. However, in starting Bible Clubs in some localities, the children are already spoiled and expect refreshments. Do not make the mistake of thinking that this situation occurs in well-to-do neighborhoods. It rather occurs in poor ones where everywhere the children go they are given something. Try to re-train them to come to Bible Club without the refreshments, but if it is impossible, do not omit them if it means having no children. Ask the Lord for His will in cases of this kind.

Question: Not one child came to my Child Evangelism Class when the day for it fell on a holiday from school, and after that the attendance was much smaller. What should I do in the future?

Answer: Your experience is quite common. When Bible Club day is a holiday, the children's schedule is upset. They always have come straight from school, and since they are not at school, they forget. Then too, the family plans outings which occupy the children. If you do desire to have a regular meeting, cards should be sent to the children to be received the day before, as this will help remind any who might otherwise forget.

Calling on the mothers the week before a holiday will be helpful. Instead of holding the class, you may dismiss it for any holidays when the children are not in school. Have that understood between you and the children. You will find, however, that sometimes the attendance will be lower afterward. The habit of coming has been broken.

The best thing to do is to choose the week when the holiday occurs for a party. During Christmas vacation when the children are apt to forget the Club meeting have a party for them. Make it a gala occasion, and talk about it much in advance. You will find it a help in getting new members for the Club, as well as keeping old members interested. Of course, you will devote a few minutes of the time to a gospel story or in some way show it is a Bible Club party. It is well to take a calendar and see what holidays fall on Thursday, if that is the day your club meets. If you inherit George Washington's birthday, you have a fine chance for a party. Thus you will not be shocked sometime when no children show up, and you discover belatedly that they were not in school. One hostess found that the party she gave during spring vacation was the beginning of real growth and interest in her class, while others who had just regular class meetings said that it marked the time when their class went downward in attendance.

Question: How can I gain the co-operation of the mothers, so that they will remind the children to come to Bible Club, and also help them with their memory work?

Answer: A friendly call from the teacher or hostess is often helpful. Besides enlisting the mother's help, the teacher gains an insight into the problems of the child and can help him in a more effective manner. Some mothers feel that the Club is set up in opposition to them and to their beliefs, and are quite antagonistic. To overcome this, one hostess wrote on each invitation before handing to the child, "Mothers always welcome." Other teachers have had special days when they invited the mothers to see just what the regular Bible Club was like. If you choose this method, be sure to pray much about that meeting as Satan seems particularly opposed to it. Mothers have had their eyes opened at these meetings and have been saved afterwards. One teacher was suddenly stricken with the flu on the day before the class when the mothers were to come, but the Lord marvellously undertook, and her sister was told not to report for work that day, and was able to make the meeting a success.

Question: Is a program with the children participating ever advisable?

Answer: Most certainly, if it is well prepared, and is typical of what the children have been doing in Bible Club. Children may give object lessons that they have had in class, presenting them in their own words; memory work may be recited; a sword drill may be conducted; songs be included; testimonies given; and even a story on the flannelgraph used. The main message may be brought briefly by an adult. One class may do this, inviting their parents and friends, or several classes may combine. If the latter is chosen, one person should direct the program, and plan what each class should do in order that the program has unity but no repetition. Great care must be exercised not to have it too long or to have it drag. Make it clear that all cannot take part. Have the children pray for the results of the program and you will find that they are very interested. Opportunity may be given at such a meeting for the friends of the work to help in a financial way. In some cases this might not be advisable. A yearly program will cause a great deal of interest and help the cause of

the Child Evangelism classes immensely, if it is conducted in the proper manner.

Question: Is it possible to train children to give an object
lesson or flannelgraph talk in their own words,
or must I write it out for them and have them
memorize it?

Answer: Do not permit them to memorize it, but
see that they are so familiar with it that they can
speak easily in their own words. To do this, several
steps should be followed.

1. Select the story, object lesson, or flannelgraph story far
    in advance.
2. Tell it in the regular course of events, not mentioning
    that it is for a program.
3. Decide in your own mind several children who might
    do it well, but do not tell them lest they become hurt
    if they are not chosen.
4. At a subsequent meeting ask one of the possibilities
    to review the story using objects or flannelgraph just
    as you did.
5. Give other children the same opportunity, and select
    the child who does it most acceptably (unless there is
    another reason why one child should give it).
6. Ask selected child to prepare it more thoroughly for
    the next class meeting.
7. Invite some other group or an adult to the class and
    let the child know in advance that he is to give the
    story for them.
8. Last of all, tell the child he is to give it on a program,
    and give him one or two more opportunities for prac-
    tice, with special help, if needed.

Why should we proceed this way? Because if a child
is informed that he is to tell a story before an adult
audience he immediately gets stage fright, and cannot
think of words even in practice. When he has already
given the story many times, he is more confident,

and it is easier for him to think of another audience. Then too, this makes it easier for the teacher to select the proper child without having to hurt someone's feelings. If more than one child is to be used, the practice may be the same. One child may put the pictures on the flannelgraph board, another may tell the story. Five- and six-year-old children have been taught in this way to give object lessons in loud, clear voices in their own words, which was much more effective than a short memorized speech. One little girl, in telling the black page of the wordless book said, "Everybody has done wrong; all the mamas and the papas and the sisters and the brothers and the aunties and the uncles, and the grandmas and the grandpas, the babies too." It was her own idea, and was much more effective than if she had stumbled through a memorized speech. We have found that the audience is tremendously interested when the children give a program in their own words. They are amazed to find what can be done with children.

TENT MEETINGS

Every summer brings with it a crop of tents which spring up like mushrooms all over the country. And every evening sees groups of adults gathered in these tents while the morning shows to all an empty tent with children nearby who need the gospel. There is no child who is not to some extent fascinated by a tent, be it a pup tent or circus tent. Why not fill the tent in the mornings with these eager boys and girls? Make it pay double dividends. And very often the harvest reaped in the morning will exceed that gathered in the evening.

For twenty years several Swedish churches on the south side of Chicago banded together for tent meetings, and for twenty years nothing was done for the children. Then the twenty-first year, evangelistic meetings were held in the mornings for the children, and nearly a hundred came to know Christ as Saviour. Mr. E. G. Winstedt, chairman of the tent committee, said, "I consider these meetings of the children to be our greatest missionary effort in all these twenty-one years of tent meetings."

Tent meetings for children may be carried on much as a Child Evangelism Class or Bible Club, with the difference of meeting daily. To follow this plan only a pianist, secretary, song leader, and storyteller are needed. Even these may be reduced by one person doing double duty. The children may be held for an hour to an hour and a quarter. A great deal may be accomplished in such a meeting, but there is little opportunity for memory work, for extensive personal work, or for personal contact between teacher and child.

Children's tent meetings may also be conducted similar to Daily Vacation Bible Schools by keeping the children two hours and omitting the handwork, which is impractical in a tent.

Sample Program

9:30-10:00	Games for those who come early
10:00-10:05	March into tent. Flag salutes
10:05-10:45	Music period, object lesson, announcements
10:45-11:20	Classes for memory work
11:20-12:00	Closing session with message, story, and invitation

The variety of such a program enables the children to give their attention for a longer period of time. This more than doubles the effect of the meetings. By devoting class periods to memory work, some inexperienced teachers may be used who would not be capable of leading children to Christ. Since the children receive the gospel and the invitation in the main meetings this is not absolutely necessary in the classes. Of course, the more experienced and the more evangelistically inclined your teachers, the better it is. However, it is possible to conduct a tent meeting without a complete staff of experienced teachers.

The teachers should meet several times beforehand to have outlined to them the purpose, plan, and program of the meetings. This is absolutely necessary if the times with the children are to proceed smoothly. Every detail should be considered and decided upon in advance. Too much planning in the spirit of dependence upon the Lord is not possible.

Expenses may be kept to a minimum. Some awards will be needed for perfect attendance, memory work, or other contests, but may be kept very simple. A final program on a Friday night, with an offering from the adults, added to the children's daily offerings, should meet the expenses.

There is an endless amount of work in conducting tent meetings for children, but souls may be saved and boys and girls established in the Word of God with the help of the Lord.

BIBLE CAMPS

The appeal of the out-of-doors life in camp has in the last few years been used as another method of reaching boys and girls with the gospel. Glowing reports as to its effectiveness in changing lives for Christ have come from those who have had children at camp.

In order to start a camp for children, a site should be selected: one that is pretty, on a lake or river for swimming, high enough in case of rain, having pure drinking water, and yet not too far from transportation. Some rent camp sites for ten days or two weeks with all the equipment available, while others prefer to build their own camp. Tents or cabins housing from eight to twelve children and one leader are best. A camp site is very important. Be sure before you select it that you are getting the features you desire.

The personnel of the staff should consist of a Camp Director, cook and kitchen crew (some older children may be permitted to earn their way as helpers at so many hours per day), life guard, with a leader for each eight or twelve children. The leaders should be able to serve double duty as handicraft teacher, Bible study teacher, pianist, or song leader. Each leader should be responsible for his set of children, checking their clothing when they arrive and leave, seeing that they obey the rules of the camp, and seeking to be used in the life of the child.

The program should be planned well in advance with nothing left to the last minute, for a well-planned program does much to put over a camp. A group of boys and girls let loose outside is not a camp; it is a dreadful mistake. Many different programs might be planned, but the following is given just as a sample and thought stimulator.

Sample Program

6:30	Reveille
7:00	Breakfast
7:30	Devotions by groups around breakfast table
8:00	Clean-up
8:30	Inspection, with banner for group with neatest tent or cabin
9:00-11:30	Morning sing, classes, message
11:30	Mail and free time
12:00	Dinner
1:00- 2:00	Rest (should be enforced)
2:00- 4:00	Recreation (Planned games, hikes, baseball, tennis, swimming, nature study)
4:00- 5:00	Handicraft
5:00- 6:00	Free time
6:00	Supper
6:30	Canteen (Candy and pop store open)
7:00- 8:00	Program (Stunt night, campfire, missionary program, etc.)
9:00	Taps and lights out

At one camp all members are sent into the woods alone with their Bibles for fifteen minutes before breakfast. In each group of eight or ten an impromptu leader is appointed who leads the members as each contribute a thought or verse from their own meditation. This gives a point and purpose to their Bible reading.

A good story around the campfire after a few songs captures the magic of the hour, and opens hearts for the message to follow.

Hold evening group devotions outside with members in a circle, arms around shoulders, and eliminate the tendency to snuggle under covers.

The last Sunday have a communion service at sunrise on a nearby hilltop. Follow with an outdoor breakfast.

At one of last campfires have a fagot service. Campers take fagot, give their testimonies, and throw fagot on the fire. Or, form a circle around the fire and as a camper gives his testimony he steps closer to the fire, forming an inner circle of those who are saved.

Divide campers into groups at the beginning of camp, naming them after Indian tribes, colleges, or even colors. Have a camp-long contest between groups, awarding points on notebooks, memory work, sporting events, etc. Have a special treat for the group that wins, such as an all-day trip, or something of special interest. Award the greater percentage of points on memory work so that it will be impossible to win unless the memory work is learned.

A few miscellaneous hints may prove valuable to the one having a camp for the first time. If possible, have the boys and girls at a different time at camp, as it will do away with many problems. Instruct children to have all clothing and possessions marked with indelible ink before coming to camp. Keep a lost and found bureau, perhaps making the child do some duty around camp to earn his article back. Limit the amount a child may spend at the canteen to eliminate stomach aches. Have some one in charge of first aid with simple remedies on hand, and the address of a good doctor on record. Accidents do happen, and it is better to be prepared. The children should be warned and instructed about any hazards such as poison ivy.

Pray much about your camp, and if possible, gather the leaders together for prayer and counsel once a day, and you will find many difficulties ironed out. Bible camps for children are comparatively new, and therefore there is much pioneering to do in this field. Why not do a little work in it yourself? You will find that it is work to a great extent, but blessing pressed down and running over. The children will never forget their time at camp, and many may be led to Christ.

As to the expense, many give the Christians an opportunity to send a boy to camp, not necessarily designating the particular boy. Others raise most of the amount beforehand, and let the children pay a nominal fee. Some raise all the money, and the children must learn five hundred Bible verses as entrance fee to camp. Some even permit the children to bring certain foodstuffs as part payment, though this involves many problems. There are as many ways of handling the expenses as there are camps. Trust in the Lord to supply the needs and proceed as He directs.

JUNIOR CHURCH

In many places the nursery at church serves a real purpose by enabling mothers with very small children to attend the church services, while in other places it has degenerated into a free-for-all for older children. In the latter case, and in the case where the majority of children leave the church as soon as Sunday school is over, a Junior Church is very much in order. But in the very rare case where all the Sunday school attendants, including the children, remain for the morning service, the Junior Church would be undesirable. Once a month Junior Church might attend in a body the opening part of the church service, and less frequently, the whole morning service. This would help train them in the importance of attending church.

The Junior Church should embody more dignity than the Sunday school. The use of more hymns than choruses, older children as ushers both for seating and for taking the offering, will add to this. A child too, may read the Scripture lesson, others may review the Sunday school lesson. Many other suggestions may be utilized from those under the chapter on Child Evangelism Class and Bible Club Hour. A few of the less hilarious drills under memory work may be employed, but the time should be kept in a more serious vein than the Sunday school. A different room than used for these same children in Sunday school is desirable, but if one is not available, a different arrangement of the furniture helps to change the atmosphere.

The Junior Church should never be used to draw children away from the morning worship, but rather prepare them to better take part in it. A certain age limit should be set depending on local conditions, and children over that limit expected to attend the adult service.

If you see the need for a Junior Church, consult your pastor and lay before him a few well-thought-out plans. He will be glad to assist you in its organization if it would be of advantage to your church.

DAILY VACATION BIBLE SCHOOL

This most worthy development in children's work has unlimited possibilities and advantages. Many suggestions given in this book will be helpful and can be incorporated into the Bible School, but to adequately cover the subject a separate volume would be required. A few suggestions follow.

The Bible School is generally of two or three weeks duration, although one week schools are profitable. Some hold them as long as six weeks. If a school is well conducted the children will not tire of it. It is a question as to how much time the teachers can devote to it.

Personnel

Only those who are saved and interested in leading children to Christ should teach in the Daily Vacation Bible School. If you have only a few spiritual Christians, use other Christians in places of minor importance as secretary, pianist, or assistant. It is of utmost importance that the ones who teach the Bible classes should be spiritual Christians with as much training as possible. The following is a list of teachers and officers necessary.

Superintendent	In charge of the whole school. The planning and greater part of the preparation is up to him. This should begin as early as January or February, and all material on hand at least a month before the school. He conducts advance sessions for teachers.
Pianist	Should be able to play hymns and choruses well.
Secretary	Should be methodical, absolutely dependable.
Teachers for each of the classes	Should be able to use flannelgraph. Regular in attendance.

Assistant for each teacher	Takes attendance, h e a r s memory work, helps keep order, assists her teacher generally.
Director of Games	In charge of children before school begins. (Not absolutely necessary.)

There may be doubling up on the responsibilities. The pianist may teach, the secretary may be director of games, etc.

Division of children into classes

Pre-school	Beginners
1st, 2nd, and 3rd grades	Primary
4th, 5th, and 6th grades	Juniors
7th and 8th grades	Intermediates
9th, 10th, 11th, and 12th grades	Seniors

Classes should be kept between twenty-five to thirty pupils unless the teacher has extraordinary ability. If fifty children come the first day in the Primary class, divide them into boys and girls, providing a new teacher and assistant. Or they may be divided by grades, having three Primary classes. There is always less of a showing in the older classes but they do not mind so much if the other classes are somewhat the same size. Even if the fifth grade had two classes, one of boys and one of girls, it would not so badly outnumber the Intermediates composed of both boys and girls. The classes must be divided in the best way that suits the given community and the teachers available. If the schools are smaller, more grades may be put together. Divide according to grades instead of years because the public school has already done the sifting process, and the ability and intelligence of the children will be much more uniform.

Curriculum

The material taught the children should not only be scriptural but evangelistic, so that the teachers may use it to lead the children to Christ. The rest of the program may be planned by the superintendent, or complete outlines for D. V. B. S. may be purchased. These may be followed exactly or altered to suit the circumstances of your school.

Contests

The following are suggestions for contests to run in the D. V. B. S. A large award board may be prepared from plywood covered with black cambric, with the awards mounted attractively. Also include on a typewritten sheet the instructions for obtaining each award. Cover the whole with cellophane. You will find that this will greatly encourage the effort of the pupils.

Perfect Record Contest	For each one who started on or before the third day, if they have a perfect record in attendance, memory work, offering, and Bible. Penny portions should be supplied those with no Bibles.
Memory Work Contest	Award to be given to the best one in each class. For large classes second and third awards may be given.
Handwork Contest	Award to be given to the best work in each class. Second and third may be given.
Storytelling Contest	Same as above.

Care must be taken to keep careful records, with absolute fairness in all contests.

Handwork

Handwork is valuable if it has on it the Word of God, but much valuable time is wasted on mere busy work. If the children have not had school with hand-work before, they will be content without it. Hand-work causes the greater part of expense of the school, more headaches for the teachers, and many discipline problems. The children do love it, and it attracts them to the school. If you can't have a school with handwork have one without it, substituting many drills and other expressional activities to take its place. The children won't miss it unless they've had it before. Many valuable projects can be worked out in the handwork period if the money and teachers are available. Handwork does have a place, but its place is not the most important on the program.

Recess

If recess is eliminated, so is much rowdiness in the classes that follow. The moving from room to room and the change of subject matter provide enough relaxation for the children. If it is desirable to have outdoor games, appoint a leader and let them take place half an hour before the school starts. This also does away with late-comers.

Expense

The ideal way is for the church to provide for the D. V. B. S. in its budget, but this is the exception rather than the rule. The Sunday school may be persuaded to finance it. Lacking this, an offering may be taken each day, with a program on the final night and offering from the audience.

Sample Schedule

This may be altered to meet the varying needs of your school.

8:55   March in to school

9:00   Worship service, all classes together.
           Salute to the flags
           Opening hymn (same hymn each morning)
           Song service
           Announcements
           Prayer chorus
           Prayer
           Object lesson or chalk talk

9:35   Classes. Bible lesson on flannelgraph, invitation, memory work

10:20   Drills, object lesson by children, recitation of memory work

10:45   Handwork or expression period

11:30   Dismissal

8

THE TEACHER AND DISCIPLINE

IT IS nine-fifteen on Sunday morning at the First
Church of Centerville, when the door to the
Primary Department opens. In comes Johnny
Rodgers, freshly attired in a blue Sunday suit, with
a pert blue cap to match. A quick glance at the neatly
arranged room tells him that he is the first one there.
He tosses his new hat toward the brightly painted
clothes rack, but misses, and the hat falls on the floor.
He runs over, picks it up, and hangs it on a hook.
Next, he looks around the room for something to
break the monotony of the silence. Ah, there is the
piano. His face bursts into a wide smile revealing a
large blank space big enough for two teeth, and he
quickly walks over to the musical instrument. Up
goes the lid, and down go the keys. Johnny needs no
Sunday school teacher to amuse him.

In the midst of terrific thunder and lightning
manufactured by musical Johnny, the door opens
again. "Hi, Bob. Come on over. Teacher's not here
yet." Bob comes on over, and the lightning and
thunder output is multiplied by two.

A few minutes later, Marjorie, Jack, and Allan
walk in, breathless from running. "I touched you
last," says Marjorie to Allan.

"Ha, ha, I got you then," and he reaches over and
gives her a shove which knocks her into a chair. Not

to be outdone, Marjorie jumps up and chases him around the table, leaving a trail of upset chairs behind her. As their game grows in excitement, the room grows more and more disorderly. The other children who come in join either the racket at the piano, or the mad game of tag.

Suddenly the door opens, and in bursts the teacher at nine-thirty-one. "Children, children, what does this mean?" She picks up an overturned chair from her pathway, and hurriedly removes her wraps. "What terrible conduct! What can you be thinking of?" And her first words to the children on Sunday morning take the nature of a scolding.

In reality, the terrible conduct was not in the children at all, but in their teacher. Of course, she excused herself to the superintendent, telling him that the boys and girls in her class were very ill-mannered. "I was only one minute late, and there was a regular mad-house in progress. It took almost the whole period to get them quiet."

Of course, those children in the foregoing incident should not have acted as they did, but there was nothing for them to do. "An idle mind is the Devil's workshop" for older people, and it is even more true for children. They are at the age in life when they have almost boundless energy. They are all action, and must be doing something. If we do not like the channel their action follows, it is up to us to place a different course before them.

> Folks say we do a lot of things
> We hadn't ought-a had
> We never mean a bit of harm,
> Nor do them to be bad;
> But when a chance just comes along

With fun a-peekin' through
We take it mostly just because
We've nothing else to do.

Boys are an awful problem
All the grown up people say—
But honest all we really want
Is just a chance to play.
And all us boys from country towns
And from the cities too,
Would quit what you call mischief
If you showed us what to do.

This situation illustrates the negative side of another proverb that every good disciplinarian must practice: "An ounce of prevention is worth a pound of cure." Too many people begin to wonder what to do about discipline problems after it is too late. The time to face behaviour difficulties is before their occurrence.

BE EARLY

"Teachers should always be on time" is a false statement. A teacher who wishes to maintain good order should never be on time; she should be early. For the first ones to arrive, whether in a Sunday school, a Child Evangelism Class, Daily Vacation Bible School, or Tent Meeting, set the atmosphere for the service. If the teacher values this atmosphere, she should be present early enough to control it.

But how are we to break down life-long habits of tardiness which are so deeply ingrained in the lives of many teachers? One method is to have a pre-prayer service for them which begins one-half hour before the children's meeting.

Perhaps you are thinking, "Oh, we couldn't have a pre-prayer service—not that early. My teachers are always late; we couldn't possibly get here that soon." But if the matter is presented in the right manner, stressing the value of prayer, rather than the need of punctuality, the teachers who are earnest and sincere will be willing to co-operate. In one Sunday school there was a teacher who was habitually from five to fifteen minutes late. Even if the Young People's Society were having a wiener roast, they expected Maybelle to be the last to arrive. However, even Maybelle made up her mind that she would attend the pre-prayer service, and she did. We saw real transformation in that whole department due to the fact that the teachers were present to greet the pupils as they came, and the minds and hearts of the teachers were quieted before the beginning of their task.

It is not only in the Sunday school that this service is valuable. In the Child Evangelism Class, where the only adults are the hostess and teacher, time can be set apart to have prayer together before the gathering of the children. Even if the hostess acts as the teacher, the necessary things may be done in advance, and the last few minutes before the meeting spent in quietness and prayer. The staff of the Daily Vacation Bible School, the group helping with the children's Tent Meeting, and any group of adults working with children will find real profit in the pre-prayer service. Not only will they find answers to their prayers, but they will learn the first rule of good discipline—"be early."

BE PREPARED

An early teacher is a wise one, but if in addition she is a prepared teacher, we have a very pleasing combination. Not only should the lesson be prepared, but the whole service should be planned. If there are songs to be sung, or Scripture passages to be read, let this be determined upon before the actual meeting. All decisions of this sort should be made and the program firmly in the mind of the leader in order that the pause—that breeding spot for discipline problems—be eliminated. For it is in such a pause that little Johnny feels an uncontrollable urge to poke the pal beside him, which, strangely enough, is followed by a stronger urge born of the spirit of retaliation which sweeps over the little pal. All of which is not conducive to the composure of the teacher.

If there are supplies to be used in the meeting, be sure that they are available at the needed time. Nothing is so advantageous to mischief as the time when teacher has to leave the room. Of course, if an emergency does arrive, and she needs something she had not anticipated, little Johnny will be less troublesome if he is sent after it, rather than left to entertain the rest. Children must be occupied every minute and it is the teacher's task to see that such occupation adds to instead of subtracts from the effect she wishes to produce. In other words, foresighted preparation is one sure way to avoid using the "pound of cure."

BE INTERESTING

Be early, be prepared, but be sure to be interesting. A child will willingly spend hours doing some-

thing in which he is interested. Why not loosen up
a trifle, and make our programs interesting for them?
It won't hurt us. It is not necessary for our lessons
to be as dry as a dust storm in order to be effective.
The gospel means "good news." Let us treat it as
such, remembering that an interested child is a good
one.

Material to be interesting should be on the right
level—easily comprehended and yet not too simple.
In a thickly populated area in Chicago, a Child
Evangelism Class was taking the neighborhood by
storm. The attendance mounted and mounted, until
sixty to sixty-five were present. The whole neighborhood was being reached. Then suddenly, with a
change of teachers, the attendance dropped more
suddenly than it had risen, with ten to twelve little
hoodlums holding the fort alone. What was the
cause? The teacher insisted on teaching the children
memory work they had already memorized. As it was
not interesting, the majority dropped out, and those
who remained were inattentive. If you find that the
children already know what you had planned to
teach and you can add no new thoughts or methods,
for discipline's sake change to something that is less
familiar. The Bible is full of stories and lessons: no
adult has ever fathomed its depths, much less a little
child.

When you see Marjorie and Allan begin to look
languidly toward the window, inject into your story
an illustration from child life. Choose an actual child,
with an actual name, the very same age as the children you are addressing, and watch their interest
deepen. In telling that wonderful Passover story, and
the salvation or destruction of the first-born, remem-

ber that some of the children in your audience are the oldest ones in their families, and that the story will really live for them if this point is brought out. There are many places in Scripture where facts of interest to children are mentioned. The little girl whom Christ raised from the dead was twelve years of age. Some in your audience may be twelve. The little boy who gave his lunch to Jesus is not so different from the boys and girls you know who have carried their lunches. You will always find that children love the familiar: stories about other children come in this category. When you are illustrating a spiritual truth, see that a child is in the illustration. Little stories about children are printed in leaflets, and are available at a very low cost. In addition to these tried and proved morsels, any incidents from actual experience are always appreciatively devoured.

BE WISE

An interesting teacher should not find difficulty in being a wise one. And it does take a wise adult to deal with a large group of modern youngsters. If we could go back a few years into our own childhood, it would help us to understand the attitudes of the children with whom we deal. Do you not remember how you looked up to a certain child in your neighborhood, and how that a suggestion from that small general decided coming activities for the whole gang? And do you not remember with what glee you exulted together when you had "put something over" on the teacher? I am sure that if you are human, you have such recollections. Even though times have changed, we know that human nature has not; leaders still remain among children, and they still feel a barrier between them and adults. It is with these leaders that most teachers have their difficulty. The children are little angels when Johnny is not present, but if he is there class might as well be dismissed for all that will be accomplished. The teacher has one objective in view, the child leader another, and the result is not gratifying to the teacher. Let us put our objective in the minds of these leaders, and get them to lead the children to do what we want them to do.

In a tent meeting for children we instructed each teacher on the very first day to choose the boy in her group whom she thought would be the naughtiest, and to bestow upon that young man the high order of captain. Some of the good ladies were shocked to think that we would thus reward badness, but we carefully explained that this was not a reward, but merely an "ounce of prevention." It was the heavy responsibility of all captains to keep the children out of the tent before the meeting, to line up the boys and girls in their group for the march, and to help maintain good order in the class while the teacher was teaching. One teacher was particularly doubtful about the wisdom of this plan. She was sure that it would take her more than one day to decide on the naughtiest boy in her group. We told her she must make the decision the first day, and that if she were alert she could discover the best captain.

After the first morning she came to us and said, "My, I didn't know it would be so easy to pick the worst one. Frank is his name; I had him spotted in the first five minutes. I told him he was to be captain tomorrow, that we would have a badge for him, and he was thrilled with the idea. Why, before that he was poking the boys beside him, while he alternated kicking and pulling the hair of another boy in front of him." But our teacher was still dubious. "He's so bad, do you think he will really make the others be good?"

The next few days told the tale. Frank took his job seriously. If some child came into the tent before time, he was bodily ejected by the determined little officer. We did not always approve his ferocious methods, but we had to admit that the results were admirable. He was present every day, arriving long before the other children, and remaining until the last teacher had departed. In between his official duties he managed to learn a great deal of memory work, and gloried in the acquisition of gold stars which were awarded for each verse. One day he astonished us by taking a younger boy aside and teaching him the Bible verse for the day. So thoroughly was he won over to the teachers' side, that one morning as we started our pre-prayer service we heard him call vociferously to the noisy group outside, "Sh, they're praying."

At the close of the meetings when the teachers were evaluating the results, one teacher remarked, "The discipline problems were rather disappointing: we didn't have any." It was remarkable considering that the neighborhood was a very rowdy one.

Yes, the children must be won over to the side of the teacher if discipline problems are to be avoided. Sometimes this may be done by singling out the leader, as in the above case, and sometimes the whole group must be won. Surprise is an excellent way to accomplish this. My aunt, who is a school teacher, was leading her class in choral reading one afternoon. The girls were fine, but the boys were about as expressive as fence posts. After wheedling, coaxing, and threatening, she said severely, "Boys, march to the hall. I want to speak to you there." Filled with curiosity, and not a little foreboding, the boys marched. As soon as the door was shut, they grouped in front of her, wondering what was the next command to be given.

"Each one of you run down the hall to the fountain, get a drink, and hurry back, but don't you dare tell the girls what we did." Three minutes later fifteen grinning boys read their lines perfectly. They were on the teacher's side.

Surprise may also take the nature of a rebuke. I well remember the first class of little children I ever had. I was so anxious to win the love of those seven and eight-year-old children that I was very soft-hearted. Jimmy always wanted to sit by delicate, dark-haired Louise, but when he did I received no attention from either one. One day, Jimmy was seeking to have the chair next to his little girl friend, but that chair was occupied; its owner believed that possession was nine points of the law. After a real mental struggle, I completely separated Jimmy and Louise, putting him on one end of the line of chairs, and Louise on the other. Walking home that day, I remember the sick feeling I had. They wouldn't like me now, I knew. But to my utter amazement, the following morning Jimmy brought me a beautiful red rose. I had not earned his ill will, but his respect.

BE PRAYERFUL

These little hints will prove helpful, but even they will not solve every discipline case. However, we do have a Saviour who can solve every problem, and we also have the privilege of taking even the behaviour of problem children to Him in prayer. But if we are going to pray about the discipline, let us not wait until the problems arise. Let us ask for wisdom in their prevention. A few adults sitting in strategic points will very often keep trouble from arising. Let all those who help with the meeting by playing the piano, taking the roll, or whatever they may do, sit in a group of children when they are not occupied with their duties. The first few meetings are very important as far as behaviour is concerned, for they set the standard for the days to follow. Every effort should be made to see that the group is orderly and well-behaved the first four times, and after that the children will accept orderliness as the standard of conduct. The converse is just as true: if the first four meetings are disorderly, you may be assured that the others will be very similar. Concentrate your prayers and efforts on the first few meetings, and be thankful that you have Someone to whom you may appeal in the hard places.

BE A SOUL WINNER

Our most important "Be" for the teacher desiring good behaviour on the part of her pupils is Be a Soul Winner. Salvation changes the behaviour of even a naughty boy. One summer, in the stockyards section of Chicago, Mrs. Warren was attempting to hold a Daily Vacation Bible School for the children.

I say "attempting" advisedly, for thirteen-year-old
Gus was determined that this was all it should be.
He sat in the back of the room, quarrelled with the
older boys, teased the younger ones, and yelled at the
teacher at intervals. For three meetings she tried to
be patient. After his success in balking her every
effort to restore order, she said to the other teachers,
"I'll give him one more chance. If he is the same
tomorrow, out he goes, and I don't care what anyone
says." Tomorrow came, and with it the unceasing
activities of Gus were resumed. The teacher also
continued with her seemingly fruitless teaching, that
day presenting to the eye the work of Christ upon
the cross. A large red heart was placed upon the
flannelgraph board and in the heart were placed the
sins common to childhood: lying, stealing, cheating,
pride, selfishness, and greed. The love of Christ was
proclaimed, and in a few words Mrs. Warren told
the story of the Cross. Then on a large cross the sins
from the heart were placed, while Mrs. Warren
explained that Christ was bearing the punishment
for our sins when He died there. As Gus was in the
very act of pulling the chair out from under the chap
in front of him, the truth of the message seemed
suddenly to dawn upon him. "Did that guy, Jesus,
do that for me?" he asked in a husky voice. Mrs.
Warren assured him that He had. "You know, I *like*
that guy, Jesus." His reply surprised everyone in
the room including himself. After the service, he
stayed and talked with his teacher, and Mrs. Warren
had the great joy of leading her greatest problem to
the foot of the Cross. Needless to say, he was no
problem after that. Salvation changes behaviour. Be
a soul winner!

You teachers who are having problems with order in your classes, evaluate yourselves. Just where is it that you are falling down? Notice again the important "Be's"—Be Early, Be Prepared, Be Interesting, Be Wise, Be Prayerful, and Be a Soul Winner. Give your earnest attention to these points in which you are weak, and you will have the joy of seeing your discipline problems minimize in importance. Discipline, you see, is not dependent upon having a group of well-mannered children, but in having a teacher who meets the problems before they arise, one who has always with her the "ounce of prevention."

9

BUILDING ATTENDANCE

A LARGE attendance is not everything. Some of the most gracious and spiritual meetings have been small ones, and some have had the most far-reaching results. One gathering was so small because of the fierce weather that even the preacher did not arrive, but that morning saw born into the family of God a mere lad who was to shake the islands of Britain, and leave them closer to his Saviour. For that morning a stumbling lay preacher had said, "You on the back seat—you look miserable, why don't you look. Look to the Cross and live." And Charles Haddon Spurgeon had looked and lived.

"For where two or three are gathered together in my name, there am I in the midst of them" (Matt. 18:20).

A purity of fellowship, a deeper insight into the individual's problems, and a more personal touch, are generally at their best in the small meeting, so let us see that we do not despise it. "Little is much if God is in it." Little children who braved the elements and struggled through drifts of snow have been turned away, and told that there will be no meeting because more did not come. What a shame! Some of the Bible's best sermons had but an audience of one. And the One who preached to Nicodemus, the Pharisee, and the woman at the well was none other than Jesus Christ Himself.

On the other hand, let us not excuse our lack of prayer and effort on these grounds. There are many without the gospel, and we should do our utmost to see that they have an opportunity to hear. Building attendance is one way to get the gospel out. It is that more may have the chance to hear, that this chapter has been written.

BY PRAYER

Prayer is the first and foremost answer to the problem of attendance. Since "it is not the will of your Father in heaven that one of these little ones should perish," surely He will answer when He is called upon to bring them in. Often prayer is the only means that will build attendance. Satan is on the warpath. Perhaps he has poisoned the mind of an influential member of the community against your group, and the children are conspicuous by their absence. Appeal to the Lord in prayer. He who has stopped the mouths of lions can undertake in your case. "He is able to do exceeding abundantly above all that you ask or think." Spread out your case before Him, as Hezekiah spread out his letter, and He will still give peace and comfort, and results. Later in this chapter different methods of increasing attendance will be given, but none are intended to replace prayer. Seek His face in regard to which methods should be employed, as some do not work in certain circumstances. He knows this before you ever begin, and can guide you in the use of the most effective weapons against inattendance. Classes which seemed to have as their permanent average four, five, or six, have suddenly skyrocketed to twenty-five or thirty when backed by consistent prayer. The teacher may pray by herself, or she may ask her friends to pray as a testimony to His power. Therefore we may make His answer a testimony by asking for prayer before the answer is seen, that more hearts may glorify God. Of all the suggestions given in this chapter, the most sure method is by prayer.

BY PERSONAL INTEREST

"My Mommy doesn't love me. She wishes she'd never had me. She said if she didn't have so many children she could have an electric refrigerator." So confided a wistful child with sad eyes to the teacher one day after Bible Club. This teacher's heart was touched, and although the girl was no longer small, the teacher took her on her lap and gave her a good "loving." Did this little girl come back? You don't even need to ask. She was a regular attendant from then on. She knew her teacher loved her, and that was what her heart was crying out for. Let us not be so concerned with numbers that we miss the needs of the individual.

There are many ways that the teacher can show that she loves her pupils. A friendly word when they come early, a hearty smile when she meets them on the street, a colorful card on their birthday, and a tactful call on their parents will do much to evidence her love, and in the end will increase the attendance. Children particularly like to have their teacher call. She should get in the habit of calling on all visitors, absentees, and sick ones. It has been suggested that a busy teacher with a large class might phone for first absence, send a card for the second, and call for the third. Calling on prospects for the class is another method of increasing attendance. A personal call in the home will give her an understanding of the child's problems she will get in no other way. It is one way of showing her love. But this love must be sincere; it can't be pinned on just for their benefit. There are two classes you can't fool—children and dogs. They detect insincerity every time. Check up on yourself. Have you been as interested in all of your pupils as you might have been? Has a visit of measles come and gone with no word from you? What an excellent opportunity a sickness is for the teacher to inculcate in the other pupils the habit of praying for, and of being kind to those who are unfortunate. Show a personal interest in each one of your pupils and visitors, and you will find it a big help to building attendance.

BY PROGRAM

No one enjoys going week after week to some meeting where he is bored to death. And children are no exception. In one Sunday school the Junior Department was noted for its lack of pupils. Some one suggested that a contest be held to secure more new pupils. But I am afraid that had a contest been held, the new pupils would have gone the way of the old ones, for on Sunday morning the superintendent of the department arrived anywhere from ten to twenty-five minutes late. When he finally arrived worship service could not be started until the adult class was petitioned for a pianist who was not a great deal of help since she didn't know the choruses familiar to the children, and they were strangers to the songs she knew. After the song service, if it could be called that, a few haphazard remarks were made on the spur of the moment, and the department was dismissed to its classes. Perhaps even then a substitute had to be sought out for one group. Such a lackadaisical organization calls not for a contest to build attendance, but for an improved program. There is no earthly use in conducting a contest and bringing in new children to such a sorry department. The first procedure is to get a consecrated superintendent with an interesting gospel-centered program that appeals to children, and they will not want to miss. If there is any contest, it should not be started until a good program has been well established.

To be interesting, a program should be varied. One plan is to divide the month by Sundays and have one teacher responsible for a certain Sunday. It might be divided this way:

1st Sunday of month	Object lesson
2nd Sunday of month	Flannelgraph talk
3rd Sunday of month	Missionary story or demonstration
4th Sunday of month	Demonstration by pupils
5th Sunday of month	Special speaker

Remember that children are interested in other children. Use them as much as possible. One Sunday school solved the problem of the destruction of hymn books by placing the most rambunctious class of boys in charge of keeping the books repaired and in order. Children may serve as ushers, may read the Scripture, may even lead the singing for their own department, if properly instructed. One child may serve as pianist and practice the songs and choruses during the week for the following Sunday. However, if after practice the songs are not played correctly,

it is better to have an adult. Make the department
as much the children's as possible, and the result will
be renewed interest. Of course, they must be impressed with the seriousness of their undertaking,
and no foolishness permitted. Other suggestions given
elsewhere in this book may be employed to give
further interest. Every minute of the program should
be planned and packed with interest in order that the
children will look forward eagerly to the service,
and will not want to miss. A good program goes a
long way in building a large attendance.

BY PROMOTION

Until the foregoing suggestions have been heard
and heeded, the ones in this section should not be
followed. A teacher who has not prayed for her class,
who does not genuinely love her pupils, and has not
painstakingly planned her program, will accomplish
nothing by trying to build attendance by artificial
methods. If, however, the foregoing suggestions have
been heeded, these ideas, under the guidance of the
Lord, may be used to a distinct advantage.

Posters

Even children can make attractive posters for use
in advertising the class or Bible school. Collect old
magazines, and clip attractive pictures from them.
These may be mounted by the children on plain or
colored cardboard, and a suitable caption printed
below. Some time ago there appeared in color the
picture of a freckled-faced girl calling "Mom's crying again, Dad." Why not mount that picture and
caption, and put underneath, " 'Cause she's too big
to go to Bible school." Then follow with the place,

date, and time of the Bible school. A picture of a
colored boy eating watermelon could be captioned
thus: "This am 'most good as Bible school." Let the
children think up titles. Of course, they should be
approved before being made, as they may not be
appropriate.

Use cardboard 11x14 inches. The pictures may be
glued on. Make letters of harmonizing color of construction paper and glue on. Show card colors and
lettering pen may be used by those you think qualified. Crayons are effective for the smaller ones.

Making the posters is only a small part. They must
now be distributed. Grocery stores, bakery shops,
beauty salons and what have you, make good places
to post them. A pleasant smile and courteous word
nearly always win permission to put the poster in
the window. Ask the proprietor where to put it, or
suggest a place, but in any event see that it is placed
before you leave. A dozen or twenty such attractive
posters (only use the most attractive—place the
others in the church or meeting place) will be a constant reminder of the meetings to come.

Handbills

Posters, when coupled with novel handbills or
folders broadcast about the community, bring the
attention of the public repeatedly to your meetings.
Blotters are sometimes the medium of the advertising. Mimeograph the bills on colored paper. Choose
for the front a picture of a child or some drawing
appealing to children. Do not just give facts, but mix
in a little imagination. You are selling the idea of
your Bible school, Tent Meeting, or special meetings to the child. What does a salesman first seek to

secure? Attention! Your work is wasted if you don't get that far. Interest is next. Seek by that folder or bit of advertising to get him interested. This leads to desire. Make him not only *know* that there is to be such a meeting, but want to *come* to it. Ask yourself this question: "If a red-haired, kite-flying champ read this folder would he want to come to these meetings?" If not, then you need to revamp your material. Perhaps you are going to introduce the song "The Gospel Train," and you have purchased a regular train whistle and bell. Why not incorporate the appeal of that somewhere in your ad? Any regular fellow is interested in trains. Seek to secure in your advertisement the *attention, interest, desire,* and *decision* of your reader.

Fish Contest

Several ideas may be worked out in connection with the verse, "Follow me and I will make you fishers of men."

1. Give each child who brings one visitor a colored paper, or metal fish. (A pattern for a paper fish may be secured from a can of salmon.)

2. Make a poster with a picture of children fishing. Record each child's name below, and attach a string through a hole punched in the bottom of the poster. For each new one brought tie a fish to the string below the proper child's name. See who is the best fisherman. Awards may be given for first, second and third best fishermen.

3. For awards on attendance contest announce the following:
   - 1st prize—large goldfish in large bowl
   - 2nd prize—medium goldfish in medium sized bowl
   - 3rd prize—small goldfish in small bowl

The fish may be purchased at the beginning of the contest, fed after each meeting, named, and speculated upon as to who will be their future owners.

4. To get a live goldfish, bring five visitors (not necessarily the same day). If each one of the five visitors comes for three meetings, the contestant receives a fishbowl.

Train Contest

From a child's color book get patterns of an engine, coal car, passenger car, freight car. Cut patterns out of construction paper of various colors. Make a poster with places along the left hand side for the engines which represent those entered in the contest. If desired, a child could be present three times before an engine with his name on it was put on the poster. For each child he brought he would be allowed to choose another car to put on behind his engine. The contest, of course, would be to see who could get the longest train. A small award could be given for the one who did. After the award time at each meeting, when an assistant pastes on the new cars deserved, "The Gospel Train" song could be sung. Let the engine of the longest train blow the whistle, the next longest ring the bell. On each car should be printed the name of the child which it represents.

In all contests scrupulous care must be taken to preserve accurate records. There must be no remembering, but it must be down in black and white. Older girls sometimes make excellent secretaries, but in a contest have been known to "fudge" for their friends. Be sure that nothing like this happens.

Creating a Continuing Interest

When a child is brought to a class or Sunday school as a visitor, he helps to swell the ranks for that particular day. The child who brought him has done his part, it is now up to the teacher to see that the child comes back. He feels strange—everything is new to him. Some little picture, pin, or very small remembrance may be given to all those present for the first time. If nothing else, a song may be sung in their honor while the new ones stand. That child has come once. But statistics from certain meetings show that those who came for three times consecutively almost always became regular members, while those who came only once or twice just as frequently dropped out. The goal, then, is to get each visitor to come for three days. A very inexpensive award may be offered to those who come for "three days in a row." If one day is missed, the child must start over again. If a choice must be made between giving an award on the first day and the third, choose the third day, and it will be of more benefit to your class. But be sure to let the children know that this award is theirs if they come for two more times. By the time the three days have gone, very likely they have started learning the memory verses, and may be bringing others. In other words, they will have one-third earned, or one-half earned other awards, and will want to complete the work. This helps to insure their regular attendance, which is what you are after. It is a great value to sustain their interest. Long before one contest has closed, another has begun, and the child is so interested that he would not think of dropping out. Perhaps it has nothing to do with attendance. It might be a memory work contest, a poster project, a picnic coming up for faithful scholars, or a program to be given for the parents. In other words, to sustain interest and consequently attendance, do not completely finish one project or contest before the child is already engrossed in another. It is like reading a serial story in a magazine, you would not think of missing the next issue. Overlap contests, projects and awards, for sustained interest.

This chapter has contained the principles of securing and holding attendance. Different contests, schemes, and plans may be worked out with a little imagination and understanding of what children like. Plans are a great help, but above all do not neglect to pray, to be personally interested in each child, and to provide an appealing program.

Note: All materials, booklets, etc. (with the exception of flannelgraph boards and easels, not now being made, and flannel) may be purchased from The Moody Press, 153 Institute Place, Chicago 10, Ill.